"C. J. Hopkins is the modern ... writer, i.e. a forbidden wit who loudly says things that are obvious but Not Spoken Of in officialdom. Probably this is not a profitable life choice, but it is a hilarious enterprise, and his furious columns have increasingly become required reading as "normal" media discourse strays further and further from reality. He has also become an expert forecaster. When it comes to predicting dystopian developments in the Trump years, his essays tend to be at least two years ahead of most American commentators, seemingly calling everything from the new Red Scares to the civil unrest of the pandemic era. As with the original Samizdat writers, you don't know where he lives and don't want to know -- you just want him to keep his head down and keep writing this stuff." — **Matt Taibbi, Rolling Stone**

"Calling C. J. Hopkins a satirist is a trivialisation. It's not 'black humor' that he displays in his columns, even if the laughter always gets stuck in your throat. His essays are a perceptive and merciless analysis of desolate politics and rotten media, which is probably only possible in this humorous style, because otherwise one would immediately become desperate and depressed." — **Mathias Bröckers, author of Conspiracies, Conspiracy Theories and the Secrets of 9/11 and other international bestsellers**

"A collection of darkly satirical essays that skewer the numbskullery of Trump, his hapless political opponents, and the boneheaded warriors of the corporate media who flounder hopelessly in his wake ... the most incisive chronicle of the reign of the 45th president and Buffoon-in-Chief of the United States of America." — **Tony Sutton, ColdType**

ALSO BY C. J. HOPKINS

HORSE COUNTRY

SCREWMACHINE/EYECANDY
(OR HOW I LEARNED TO STOP
WORRYING AND LOVE BIG BOB)

THE EXTREMISTS

ZONE 23

TRUMPOCALYPSE: CONSENT FACTORY ESSAYS
VOL. I (2016-2017)

THE WAR ON POPULISM

CONSENT FACTORY ESSAYS

VOL. II (2018-2019)

C. J. HOPKINS

CONSENT FACTORY PUBLISHING

This Consent Factory Publishing trade edition September 2020.

Consent Factory Publishing is a wholly-owned subsidiary of Consent Factory, Inc., a subsidiary of Amalgamated Content, Inc., distributors of quality literary content throughout the developed and developing worlds. For more information about Consent Factory Publishing, visit the Consent Factory's website: consentfactory.org.

Cover design by Anthony Freda.

Author's portrait by Johanna Fischer.

The essays in this volume were originally published by *Consent Factory*, and then republished by *CounterPunch*, *The Unz Review*, *OffGuardian*, *ColdType*, *The Greanville Post*, *ZeroHedge*, *Dissident Voice*, *Entelekheia*, *Le Grand Soir*, *Come Don Chisciotte*, *Übersetzungen aus dem Imperium*, *Linke Zeitung*, *Mint Press News*, *Réseau International*, *Tlaxcala*, *ZNet*, *Rebelión*, *Na Severu*, *South Front*, *Burbuja*, *The Fringe News*, *Soverain*, *Contramedia*, *Brasil No Caos*, *The Duran*, *Signs of the Times*, *OpEd News*, *Titanic Lifeboat Academy*, *The Fire*, and *Information Clearing House*.

Printed in the United States of America

ISBN 978-3-9821464-1-6 (pb)

Contents

GloboCap and Its Discontents 9
The War on Dissent 19
The Spectre of Divisiveness 25
Then They Came for the Globalists 31
Jeremy Corbyn's Nazi Death Cult 37
The Simulation of Democracy 43
Awaiting the Putin-Nazi Apocalypse 49
Hardcore Hitler on Hitler in Helsinki 55
Trump's Treasonous Traitor Summit 61
Where Have All the Nazis Gone? 67
Putin-Nazi Paranoia 73
Down with the Working Classes! 79
Who Doesn't Love Identity Politics? 83
The Putin-Nazi-Terrorist-O-Matic 89
Oceania is at War with Fascism 95
The Indiscreet Charm of the Gilets Jaunes 101
The Year of Putin-Nazi Paranoia 107
The War on Populism 115
The Magic Socialist 121
Anti-Semitism Pandemic 125
Mueller-Dämmerung 131
A Russiagate Requiem 135
Democracy vs. the Putin-Nazis 139
The Hitlerization of Jeremy Corbyn 143
The United States of Fascism Hysteria 149
The War on White-Supremacist Terror 155
The Future of the Spectacle 161
Trumpenstein Must Be Destroyed! 167
Reclaiming Your Inner Fascist 173
The Year of Manufactured Hysteria 179

“If there is hope, it lies in the proles.”
— George Orwell, 1984

GloboCap and Its Discontents

September 1, 2020

The global capitalist empire never officially declared the "War on Populism." No votes were taken. No speeches were made. There were no congressional or parliamentary debates. No one got on the phone to anyone, or issued any confidential memos to anyone. The media received no press releases. There weren't even any secret meetings of the Illuminati at the Bilderberg conference, or Davos, or that creepy Masonic-looking temple on Jeffrey Epstein's island.

None of that stuff was necessary. Everyone who was anyone just intuitively knew that the war had begun, and exactly what they were expected to do. They intuited this at approximately midnight on November 8, 2016, but it would take them most of the following year to execute the official narrative changeover from the "War on Terror" to the "War on Populism."

The Intelligence agencies got right to work, fabricating dossiers, duping generals into lying to the FBI, spreading scurrilous rumors about Russian "collusion," "pee-tapes," "Russian Facebook influencers," and conducting other COINTELPRO-type ops. The corporate media also sprang into action, disseminating unprecedented amounts of disinformation, official propaganda, and anything else their contacts in the Intelligence Community gave them to disseminate.

Hysterical liberals festooned themselves with safety pins and took to the streets. A fake "Resistance" movement was launched.

Corporations started censoring the Internet.

The "terrorist" threat that had plagued the world for fifteen years disappeared overnight. A new official narrative was born. "America" and "democracy" were now under attack by a conspiracy of Russian-backed neo-fascists that had magically materialized out of the ether more or less the moment Trump won the election.

The Putin-Nazis were on the march!

Throughout the course of 2017, day after day, hour after hour, the corporate media relentlessly disseminated and reinforced the new official narrative. Western liberals bought it immediately, but it took a bit longer to threaten, guilt-trip, and otherwise mindfuck and emotionally manipulate the broader Left into going along. The Russia hysteria alone was not going to cut it, not with bitter Bernie Sanders supporters, and other such Clinton-hating leftists, many of whom considered themselves "anti-imperialists," "anti-corporatists," or at least "anti-fascists."

And this was the genius of the Putin-Nazi narrative, this two-pronged Russia-plus-Fascism approach! Whipping liberals into a mindless frenzy of Russia-hating mass hysteria was easy, but the global capitalist empire needed to win over the "anti-imperialist" Left (and the identity-politics or "identitarian" Left). So they manufactured the fascism hysteria to run alongside the Russia hysteria, and, gradually, inevitably, that did the trick.

By somewhere near the end of Trump's first year in office, the "Resistance" had successfully recruited and instrumentalized most of the Western Left in its counter-insurgency against the "populists." Russia hysteria was raging in the mainstream, and fascism hysteria was raging on the fringes. Identitarian leftists were predicting an imminent "Reichstag" false-flag event, which Trump would use as cynical pretext to impose martial law, declare himself Führer, and order his underground army of white-supremacist extremists to start murdering the Jews, or the African-Americans, or the Mexicans, or someone.

And it wasn't just Trump and his silent majority of Russia-backed American Putin-Nazis. "Populists" were coming out of the woodwork. In the U.K., there were the Brexit populists, and there was Jeremy Corbyn and his communist populists. In Germany, there was the AfD. In France, Mélenchon and Le Pen. In Italy, Salvini and Grillo. Kaczynski in Poland. Erdoğan in Turkey. Orbán in Hungary. Bolsonaro in Brazil. Morales in Bolivia. Maduro in Venezuela.

The list went on, and on, and on.

By January 2018, the "War on Populism" was in full swing. The empire (a/k/a "GloboCap") was hammering the "populists" on multiple fronts. In the minds of millions of hysterical liberals, Donald

Trump, a garden-variety narcissistic billionaire ass clown, was now both a Russian sleeper agent and literally the resurrection of Hitler. The Resistance, and its savior, Robert Mueller, were building an air-tight case against him and his Russo-Nazi co-conspirators. It was only a matter of time until they impeached him and perp-walked him out of the White House.

Meanwhile, in Great Britain, the GloboCap "Resistance" was Hitlerizing Jeremy Corbyn (who was probably also working for the Russians, although exactly in what capacity was never made clear). According to most of the British media, the Labour Party had been transformed into a genocidal neo-Nazi Death Cult. A Corbyn-led communist holocaust was imminent. The exodus of British Jews had begun ...

*

And so on. I won't attempt to capture the full extent of the insanity here. I've tried to do so in the essays that follow, which were written and published as events unfolded. Hopefully, along with Volume I of this series (2016-2017), they will provide some sort of unofficial historical record of what actually happened (and just how batshit crazy it all got) as the empire unleashed the full force of its fearsome propaganda machine to put down the growing "populist" insurgency.

This conflict, the "War on Populism" (i.e., GloboCap putting down a "populist" insurgency), is at the root of the madness of these last four years. To understand it, one needs to understand that it is primarily *an ideological conflict*, a global war for hearts and minds.

Trump, Johnson, Corbyn, Sanders, and other so-called "populist" figures, were never an actual threat to GloboCap, not in any material sense. They were always just symbols, representations of resistance to global capitalist ideology. It is this resistance to its ideology (from both the Left and the Right ... it makes no difference), more than any particular political leader or movement, that GloboCap has been working to crush. It needs to put down this "populist" insurgency, so that it can get on with the business of transforming the world into one big value-less marketplace ... which is what it has been doing for the last thirty years.

This is what capitalism was built to do. Ideologically speaking, it is a simple machine, one that strips societies of "despotic" values (i.e., values established by kings, clergies, aristocracies, political parties, communities, artists, families, et cetera) and replaces them all with a single value, exchange value, rendering everything a commodity. In essence, it is an ideological machine, a values-decoding/recoding machine, which transforms societies into markets.

This is exactly what global capitalism set out to do in the 1990s following the collapse of the USSR, first, in the former Eastern Bloc countries, and then promptly also in the Middle East. It went on a society-restructuring rampage. GloboCap did this, not the USA. The goal was not to conquer and colonize former Soviet and Soviet-aligned terrorities; the goal was to aggresively destabilize, restructure, and privatize these territories, and then absorb them into the global market.

Now, I want to be as precise as possible. What I am calling "global capitalism" is not the economic system per se (i.e., private property, capital accumulation, wage labor, voluntary exchange, and so on). I'm talking about capitalism as ideology.[1]

OK ... what *is* ideology, exactly?

There are many definitions of ideology. The definition I'm working with is basically that of Marx and Engels as set forth in *The German Ideology*,[2] the "production of ideas, of conceptions, of consciousness," everything "men say, imagine, conceive."

So, I'm not talking about ideology generally. I'm talking about the system of axiomatic beliefs, principles, and values on which a culture is based, and according to which that culture operates, and which determines how reality is perceived in that culture.

---

1 Actually, I'm talking about post-ideology. In a globally hegemonic system such as ours, ideology is rendered obsolete. Such a system has no external enemies, and thus no ideological adversaries. It has no need for ideology. Its ideology has become "normality," "reality," or "just the way it is." Likewise, all opposing ideologies are no longer regarded as challenges to the system warranting refutation and debate; they are regarded as deviations from the "norm," pathologies, to be treated, or eliminated. Religious fundamentalism is a good example of this. While everyone under global capitalism is totally free to maintain whatever religious and spiritual values they choose, they are not free to live according to such values (unless they don't conflict with global capitalist ideology). Those who attempt to do so are labelled "mentally ill," or "religious extremists," which amounts to more or less the same thing. Communism is another example. Whereas once it was perceived as an existential threat, now, it is laughed at, dismissed out of hand as "unrealistic" or "delusional" thinking.

2 Marx & Engels, The German Ideology (written 1845), The Marx-Engels Institute, 1932

I'm talking about the production of consciousness.

Ideology, in this sense, is not a lie that the ruling classes apply to reality, or something that hides or distorts reality. It is nothing less than reality itself. It doesn't only determine *what* we think; it determines *how* we think, and what we do not think, what we cannot even begin to think ... not because we are forbidden to think it, but, rather, because we are unable to imagine anything beyond the conceptual limits of the ideology that has produced our thinking.

In essence, ideology is a territory ... a territory we call "reality." Its limits are the limits of our collective imagination, the limits of our definition of "sanity." Within its limits, reality makes sense. Beyond them, there is only madness. Apostasy. Excommunication.

So, what is global capitalism's ideology?

Global capitalism's ideology (i.e., the territory that comprises our "reality") is unlike any other ideology in the 5,000-year history of ideology. It is an ideological territory without limits, neither internal nor external boundaries. It is a featureless territory, in which anything is possible, because nothing within it has any value, or meaning, in and of itself. It is literally a "desert of the real," an infinite, seamless desert of values, across the lifeless surface of which the ghosts of dead values eternally wander, in circles, aimlessly, signifying nothing, going nowhere, for they are already there, in the only place there is to be ... because the desert is everywhere, and everything.

There is nowhere and nothing outside of this territory. There is no "outside" where anything could exist. It is one big global capitalist world, one unitary, omnipresent, capitalist "reality" ... one big global marketplace, or it will be, once GloboCap finishes destabilizing and restructuring what remains of the post-Cold-War world.

This is the story of the last thirty years. Beneath the distractions of the day, the manufactured mass hysteria, the official propaganda, the fabricated outrage, the scandals, the wars, rumors of wars, the deafening roar of a billion voices shrieking gibberish at you on social media, the conspiracy theories, real and imagined, the cheap charade of electoral politics, and so on ... right out there in the open, because no one has paying it much attention, GloboCap has been mopping up, stripping societies of their non-market values, absorbing them into the global market, implementing ideological conformity.

You're familiar with this ideological conformity. We all are. You're probably in favor of many of the "values" with which it markets itself ... anti-racism, equal rights, separation of church and state, et cetera, the traditional liberal agenda. Remember, capitalist ideology is what finally freed us from the rule of despots, kings, aristocracies, priests, and the like.[3] As I explained above, capitalism did this by eradicating "despotic" values (mostly during the 18th and 19th centuries, by both revolutionary and less violent means) and replacing them all with a single value, exchange value, rendering everything a commodity.

That doesn't sound very appealing, however. No one wants to be a commodity, or live in a world without any real values. So capitalism marketed itself as "democracy," and that went over much better with the masses.

Here we are, a few hundred years later, and "democracy" (i.e., capitalism) is running out of "despotic" values to eradicate and "liberate" us from. Sure, it still has some work to do, secularizing the Middle East, and there are still a few countries that aren't playing ball, but most of the planet has gotten with the program. The majority of the values-eradicating work that remains to be done is right here at home. There are still a lot of Western consumers who haven't completely embraced "democracy," and who are clinging to old "despotic" values ... racist values, religious values, nativist values, xenophobic values, homophobic values, transphobic values, cultural and artistic values, ableist values, alloist values, shadeism, lookism, ethnocentrism, cisgenderism, anti-Semitism, jingoism, sexism, sizeism, saneism ... the list goes on and on, and on.

Democracy (i.e., global capitalism) will not rest until it has purified society (i.e., the global marketplace) of these dangerous, destructive, despotic values, and implemented a global "code of conduct" (like the ones most major corporations have) with universal "anti-hate-speech" guidelines, and "appropriate vocabulary" lists, and has erased any visible symbol of such despotic values from public view, and any references to them from school curricula, and otherwise transformed humanity into a mass of hyper-conformist consumers who all look like models in a Benetton commercial and talk like customer service representatives.

3 Personally, I'm extremely grateful for that. From the sounds of it, despotism wasn't much fun.

Now, don't get me wrong, I'm in favor of democracy, and I'm not a fan of racism or any other type of discrimination. I'm just trying to shed a little light on the forces behind the identity-politics zealotry that has been ascendant recently, and the "populist" backlash against such zealotry.

This zealotry, this crusade for ideological conformity, is described by liberals and leftists as a movement to bring about "social justice," and by conservatives as "cultural Marxism." It is neither. Or, all right, it contains elements of both, but, essentially, it is global capitalism purifying society of those despotic values, establishing that infinite, value-free, meaningless "desert of the real" which I outlined above.

Just as everything that exists within the capitalist market is of no inherent value (i.e., derives its value purely as a commodity), nothing in this "desert of the real" contains any value, or meaning, in itself, or even any essential qualities. Everything is fungible, interchangeable. People are reconstitutable units, one day this, the next day that. Identities are as casually adopted and discarded as any other article of fashion. Everywhere you go is like everywhere else, or is on its way to becoming the same. Soldiers fight for corporations. Generals answer to chartered accountants. The vicious, inbred monarchs and blue-blooded aristocracies of old are gone, replaced by a simulated aristocracy comprised of glorified widget salesmen. Marketing is the new religion. This is the limitless, meaningless world that GloboCap is bringing into being, a world where, as Hassan-i-Sabbah would say, "nothing is true; everything is permitted."

It is global capitalism (i.e., the system) that is doing this. It is not a bunch of guys in a room. It is a lot of bunches of guys in rooms, making business decisions, not ideological decisions. They don't need to worry about ideology. The ideology is built into the system. And it is the system that is in control now. Not the billionaires. Not the oligarchs. Not the bankers. Not the CEOs. The people at the top of the system are just as interchangeable as the people at the bottom of it. They are profiting from it, but they are not running it. No one is running it, because no one has to. Global capitalism is running itself. It is running everything. It is running us all, driving us mindlessly forward into a nihilistic commodified future where everything goes because nothing means anything.

*

OK, at this point, I should probably present my solution to the depressing picture I just painted. I'm sorry, but I do not have one. I do not know how to stop this train. I suspect that it is probably unstoppable. Which doesn't mean it's the end of the world. (It almost always never is.) Sometimes things need to run their course before we can conceive of what comes next. That's probably the case with global capitalism, and is probably why, despite the ridiculous nature of GloboCap's official propaganda, manufactured mass hysteria, and other counter-insurgency measures over the course of these last four years, it will eventually win the "War on Populism," and restructure and privatize the rest of the planet.

How many pockets of resistance remain (*not* resistance to the USA ... *resistance to global capitalism*, to global capitalist ideology)? How long do you imagine these pockets of resistance can resist the military, economic, and cultural pressure of a global empire determined to strip them of their outmoded values and absorb them into the global marketplace?

Not much longer, in historical terms.

These pockets of resistance to global capitalism are mostly either nationalist or fundamentalist in character, and have been proving significantly harder to restructure and absorb than the remnants of communism.[4] But GloboCap has time on its side. Neo-nationalist "populism" is not going to turn back the clock of history. Neither is religious fundamentalism. We might be heading toward some form of pathologized, corporate neo-feudalism, but we are not going back to classical despotism, despite the desire of so many to do so.

4 GloboCap couldn't possibly care less what a country like China calls itself, or what propaganda it feeds to its own people, as long as it is playing ball with GloboCap, which the People's Republic obviously is ... as are Cuba, Laos, and Vietnam. The Czech Republic. Poland. Hungary. Romania. Albania. The former Yugoslavia. The list goes on, and on, and on. Even Russia (GloboCap's official enemy du jour) is playing ball, notwithstanding the propaganda Westerners are fed. It is easy to get distracted by the competition between nation-states, but it is really no different (and no more dangerous) than that which occurs between corporations. Neither the United States nor any other major country is going to conquer any other major country. Every developed country on Earth is economically interdependent. If the United States launched a war on China, it would be attacking its own manufacturing base, or rather, GloboCap's manufacturing base.

The age of nationalism is over. No amount of reactionary kicking and screaming is going to bring it back. The neo-nationalist "populism" that has been on the rise for the last few years is not a rerun of the 1930s, or the reemergence of "literal fascism." It is the death throes of nationalism, of national sovereignty ... like the supernova of a dying star, or the violent spasms of a suffocating fish.

Not that nations are going to disappear. They will continue to exist as administrative units, marketing demographics, and simulations of democracy. And the death throes of nationalism will probably get a bit more violent before they subside, as will the general discontent with global capitalist ideology.

Despite the propaganda the corporate media have been barraging us with for the last four years, the fact is, it isn't just the "populist Right" (i.e., neo-nationalists) that are having trouble adjusting to the new global-capitalist reality. There are a lot of old-fashioned leftists who are also not too thrilled with where things are headed.

GloboCap is acutely aware of this, and is working very hard to keep these two groups of "populists" at each other's throats, mostly by racializing and genderizing everything, and otherwise using identity politics to drive a wedge through the "populist" masses (also known as the working classes). As long as they can keep the Trumpians and the Brexiters, and the Bernie Bros and Corbynistas, and the Black Lives Matterists and trans-rights militants, and the feminists, and the Christians, and Muslims, and Jews, and the neo-Confederate Boogalooists, and Antifa, and all the other identitarian subsets and sects at war with each other, any threat they pose to GloboCap is easily contained, or instrumentalized. So far, their strategy appears to be working, and there's no reason to think it won't continue to.[5]

No, short some catastrophic planetary event, like a global thermonuclear war, a devastating meteor strike, or total ecological collapse (or something else that brings an end to modern civilization as we know it), global capitalism is going to continue to remake the world into a "desert of the real." As it does this, it is going to continue to polarize and terrorize the masses into ideological conformity ... as it did throughout the two years covered in these essays.

---

5 The United States of America, for example, is teetering on the brink of a corporate-sponsored, racialized civil war at the moment.

In any event, whatever unfolds over the longer course of history, in the near term, you may want to fasten your seatbelts and restore your tray-tables to their upright positions. We're in for a bit of a bumpy ride. If the first half of 2020 is any indication of what is in store for us, you might want to get a jump on things and go ahead and adopt the "brace" position.

It is too soon to know whether the so-called "New Normal" that GloboCap has been implementing (under the guise of trying to save humanity from a virus which appears to be no more deadly, or not much deadlier, than the common flu) and the civil race war it has been trying to foment signals the end of the "War on Populism" or just a new, more totalitarian stage of it ... but that's a question for a later volume.[6]

In the meantime, let's return to those heady days of January 2018, when the shock of the "Trumpocalypse" was finally wearing off, and the "War on Populism" was just getting going, and maybe remember exactly how we got here.

Ready? All right, here we go.

---

6 I am, of course, covering these developing stories in my 2020 Consent Factory columns. The roll-out of the New Normal ideology is particularly unsettling. As I noted in a recent column, Invasion of the New Normals, August 9, 2020: "The 'New Normal' slogan has been relentlessly repeated (in a textbook totalitarian 'big lie' fashion) for going on the past six months. We have heard it repeated so many times that many of us have forgotten how insane it is ... the idea that the fundamental structure of society needs to be drastically and irrevocably altered on account of a virus that poses no threat to the vast majority of the human species. And, make no mistake, that is exactly what the 'New Normal' movement intends to do. 'New Normalism' is a classic totalitarian movement (albeit with a pathological twist), and it is the goal of every totalitarian movement to radically, utterly transform society, to remake the world in its monstrous image."

The War on Dissent

January 26, 2018

Just when you thought the global corporatocracy couldn't possibly get more creepily Orwellian, the Twitter Corporation starts sending out emails[1] advising that they "have reason to believe" we have "followed, retweeted," or "liked the content of" an account "connected to a propaganda effort by a Russian government-linked organization known as the Internet Research Agency."

While not as dramatic as the thoughtpolice watching you on your telescreen, or posters reminding you that "Big Brother Is Watching," the effect is more or less the same.

And if that's not creepily Orwellian enough for you, Facebook has launched a Ministry of Counterspeech, manned by "a dedicated counterterrorism team" of "former intelligence and law-enforcement officials," to "disrupt ideologies underlying extremism."[2]

Google is systematically disappearing, deranking, and maliciously misrepresenting non-corporate news and opinion sources and the "thoughtcriminals" who contribute to them.

Meanwhile, the corporate media continue to pump out Russia-paranoia propaganda like the recent Maddow segment on MSNBC[3] about "the remarkable number of Russian financiers who'll be rubbing elbows with the Trump team in Davos."

These are just the latest salvos in the corporate establishment's War on Dissent, an expanded version of the War on Terror, which

---

1 O'Sullivan, Donie, "Twitter to tell 677,775 people they interacted with Kremlin-linked trolls," CNN Business, January 19, 2018 ("Twitter will inform nearly 700,000 people in the U.S. that they either followed a Kremlin-linked troll account, or retweeted or liked a tweet sent by one of the accounts, the social media company said Friday.")

2 Hedges, Chris, "Thought Police for the 21st Century," Truthdig, January 21, 2018 ("Monika Bickert, head of global policy management at Facebook, told the U.S. Senate Committee on Commerce, Science, and Transportation in a hearing Wednesday that Facebook employs a security team of 10,000 -- 7,500 of whom 'assess potentially violating content' -- and that 'by the end of 2018 we will more than double' it to over 20,000. Social media companies are intertwined with and often work for U.S. intelligence agencies. This army of censors is our Thought Police.")

3 Maddow, Rachel, "Team Trump empties White House for Davos trip," MSNBC, January 24, 2018

they've been relentlessly waging for over a year now. As you may have noticed, the ruling classes have been using virtually every propaganda organ at their disposal to whip up mass hysteria over a host of extremely dubious threats to "the future of democracy" and "democratic values," Russia being foremost among them, followed closely by white supremacy, then a laundry list of other "threats," from Julian Assange to Bernie Bros to other, lesser "sowers of division."

This propaganda campaign is part and parcel of the roll-out of a new official narrative. If it wasn't so completely depressing, I would say it is awe-inspiring to watch. This full-spectrum type of mass indoctrination (or reality adjustment) doesn't happen that often. It used to only happen on the national level, typically during times of war, when the ruling classes of nation states needed to temporarily unite their populaces and demonize their enemies. It is happening now on a global level, for the second time in the 21st Century.

The first time it happened on a global level was 2001-2002, when the War on Terror narrative was launched to supplant the defunct Cold War narrative that had functioned since the end of World War II. The End of History/New World Order narrative, which had served as a kind of ideological stop-gap from 1990 to 2001, never really sold that well. It was far too vague, and there was no clear enemy. The global capitalist ruling classes (which now reigned unopposed over the entire planet) needed a new official narrative to unite, not just a nation, or region, but everyone within the new global market. This narrative needed a convincing enemy that would function on a global level.

"Terrorism" is that enemy.

In the official War on Terror narrative, the term "terrorism" does not refer to any type of actual terrorism (although of course such terrorism does occur) as much as to "terrorism" as a general concept, an essentially meaningless pejorative concept, one which can be expanded to include almost anything and anyone the ruling classes need it to ... which is what is taking place at the moment. It is being expanded, rather dramatically, to include virtually any type of dissent from global capitalist ideology.

In order to understand what's happening, we need to understand how terms like "terrorism" and "extremism" function ideologically, not just as terms to dehumanize "bad guys" but to designate a type of ur-antagonist, one that conforms to the official narrative.

So let's take a few minutes and try to do that.

The key to understanding both the original War on Terror official narrative and the expanded variation we are being sold currently is the fact that terrorism is an insurgent tactic employed by weaker militant forces against a ruling government or occupation force. This makes it the perfect bogeyman (in essence, the only bogeyman) for our brave new global capitalist world, where global capitalism takes the place of that "ruling government or occupation force."

I've written a number of essays about this,[4] so I won't reiterate all that here. The short version is, we no longer live in a world where nation-against-nation conflict is driving the course of political events. We live in a world where global capitalism is driving the course of political events. The economies of virtually every nation on the planet Earth are interdependent. Capitalist ideology pervades all cultures, despite their superficial differences. It is a globally hegemonic system, so it has no external enemies. None. The only threats it faces are internal. Its "enemies" are, by definition, insurgent ... in other words, "extremist" or "terrorist."

This even holds true for the Russia paranoia that the ruling classes are pumping out currently ... it's all just part of the reality adjustment, and the launch of the new official narrative, not a prelude to war with Russia.

The USA is not going to war with Russia. The notion is beyond ridiculous. Have you noticed, despite all their warlike verbiage, that no one has put forth a single scenario in which war between Russia and the West makes sense? That's because it doesn't make sense. Not for Russia, the USA, or anyone else. This is why "the Russian threat" is being marketed as an "attack on democratic values" and "an attempt to sow division," and so on. Because the war the corporatocracy is waging is not a war against Russia, the nation. The war they are fighting is a counter-insurgency, an ideological counter-insurgency. "Russia" has just been added to the list of "terrorists" and "extremists" who "hate us for our freedom."

---

4 Hopkins, C. J., Trumpocalypse: Consent Factory Essays, Vol. I (2016-2017), Consent Factory Publishing, November 2019

Thus, our new official narrative is actually just a minor variation on the original War on Terror narrative we've been indoctrinated with since 2001. A minor yet essential variation. From 2001 to 2016, the constant "terrorist threat" we were facing was limited to Islamic terrorism, which made sense as long as the corporatocracy was focused on restructuring the Middle East. White supremacist terrorism was not part of the narrative, nor was any other form of terrorism, as that would have just confused the audience.

That changed, dramatically, in 2016.

The Brexit referendum and the election of Trump alerted the global capitalist ruling classes to the existence of another dangerous insurgency that had nothing to do with the Greater Middle East. While they were off merrily destabilizing, restructuring, privatizing, and debt-enslaving, resentment of global capitalism had grown into a widespread neo-nationalist backlash against globalization, the loss of sovereignty, fiscal austerity, and the soulless, smiley-face, corporate culture being implemented throughout the West and beyond.

That this backlash is reactionary does not change the fact that it is an insurgency, just as Islamic fundamentalism is. Both insurgencies are doomed attempts to revert to despotic social systems (nationalist in one case, religious in the other) and so reverse the forward march of global capitalism. The global capitalist ruling classes are not about to let that happen.

The corporatocracy wasted no time in dealing with this new insurgency. They demonized and hamstrung Trump, as they will continue to do until he's well out of office. But Trump was never the significant threat. The significant threat is the people who elected him, and who voted for Brexit, and the AfD, and Sanders, and Mélenchon, and Corbyn, or who just stayed home on election day and refused to vote for Hillary Clinton. The threat is the attitude of these people. The insubordinate attitude of these people. The childish attitude of these people (who naively thought they could challenge the most powerful empire in the annals of human history ... one that controls, not just the most fearsome military force that has ever existed, but the means to control "reality" itself).

The corporatocracy is going to change that attitude, or it is going to make it disappear. It is in the process of doing this now, using every ideological weapon in its arsenal. The news media. Publishing. Hollywood. The Internet. The Intelligence agencies. Congressional inquiries. Protests. Marches. Twitter's "advisory emails." Google's manipulation of search results. Facebook's "counterspeech" initiative. Russiagate. Shitholegate. Pornstargate. Et cetera.

The ruling class is sending us a message. The message is, "you are either with us or against us." The message is, "we will tolerate no dissent, except for officially sanctioned dissent." The message is, "try to fuck with us, and we will marginalize you, and demonize you, and demonetize you, and disappear you."

The message is, "we control reality, so reality is whatever the fuck we say it is, regardless of whether it is based in fact or just some totally made-up story we got *The Washington Post* to publish and then had the corporate media repeat, over and over, for fourteen months."[5]

If that doesn't qualify as full-blown Orwellian, I'm not sure what, exactly, would.

I wish I had some rallying cry to end this depressing assessment with, but I have no interest in being one of these Twitter-based guerrilla leaders who tell you we can beat the corporatocracy by tweeting and donating to them on Patreon, and then going about our lives as "normal." It's probably going to take a little more than that, and the obvious truth is, the odds are against us.

That said, I plan to make as much noise about The War on Dissent as humanly possible, until they marginalize me out of existence … or the corporate-mediated simulation that so many of us take for existence these days.

What do you say, want to join me?

---

5 Norton, Ben & Greenwald, Glenn, "Washington Post Disgracefully Promotes a McCarthyite Blacklist From a New, Hidden, and Very Shady Group," The Intercept, November 26, 2016 ("The Washington Post on Thursday night promoted the claims of a new, shadowy organization that smears dozens of US news sites that are critical of US foreign policy as being 'routine peddlers of Russian propaganda.' The article by reporter Craig Timberg, headlined 'Russian propaganda effort helped spread 'fake news' during election, experts say,' cites a report by an anonymous website calling itself PropOrNot, which claims that millions of Americans have been deceived this year in a massive Russian 'misinformation campaign.'")

The War on Dissent Part 2: The Spectre of Divisiveness

February 16, 2018

A spectre is haunting Western democracy — the spectre of "divisiveness." After eight blessed years of peace and prosperity under the glorious reign of Obama the Benevolent, suddenly, we find ourselves besieged on all sides by Russian-sponsored sowers of "discord,"[1] disseminators of "disinformation," inculcators of "confusion" and "chaos," and other enemies of our "democratic values." These devilish instigators of "disunion" and "distrust" are determined to deceive us into doubting "the truth" by exposing us to "divisive ideas" and seducing us with their cynical skepticism into questioning the integrity of our political leaders, our intelligence agencies, and the corporate media, who would never, ever, dream of lying to us ... or so goes the new official narrative being rolled out by the corporatocracy.

It is utterly stupefying to watch as millions of Americans conform their beliefs and behavior to this official narrative like Inner Party Members in 1984. Apart from the fact that its storyline is simplistic and childish to the point of absurdity, it has only been roughly sixteen years since the corporatocracy introduced the beta version of this same official narrative, to which millions of Americans obediently conformed ... which resulted in the deaths of hundreds of thousands, the destabilization of the entire Middle East, and the transformation of most Western societies into militarized surveillance states.

As I outlined at length in part one of this essay, the War on Dissent being rolled out currently is an expansion of the "War on

1 *Jackson, Lawrence, "Russia Sees Midterm Elections as a Chance to Sow Fresh Discord," The New York Times, February 13, 2018*

Terror" narrative, the storyline of which was equally childish, and simplistic, and blatantly fabricated. Though it is fashionable these days for the politicians and corporate media propagandists who sold the "Saddam has WMDs" story, and the "Iraq is linked to al Qaeda" lie, and the "we're fighting terrorism in Afghanistan" fairy tale, to regret how they "misinterpreted the intelligence" that led to the "unfortunate blunder" that launched the global corporatocracy's occupation and restructuring of the Middle East (which continues unabated to date), anyone with half a brain could see what was really going on at the time.

You didn't have to be a rocket scientist to figure out that the "War on Terror" was not a war on terrorism (the concept is nonsensical on its face), but, rather, was just the official narrative that would allow the global capitalist ruling classes to (a) employ the United States military to pursue their aims throughout the world with more or less complete impunity, and (b) designate anyone opposing the hegemony of global capitalism a "terrorist."

Several million of us figured that one out ... or at least figured out that the U.S. government, the Intelligence community, and the corporate media were using Americans' emotional response to the September 11 terrorist attacks to con us into supporting the invasion and destabilization of the Middle East for reasons that had nothing to do with terrorism.

So we did what Americans are taught to do. We peaceably assembled to petition our government, as did millions of people across the world, and otherwise raised as much ruckus as we could about how folks were being manipulated ... and were denounced as "traitors," "terrorist sympathizers," and "conspiracy theory nuts" for our efforts. And not just by the corporatocracy, also by regular Good Americans.

All these years later, knowing what we know, you might assume that all those Good Americans who rushed out to buy American flags to wave as our troops destroyed a country that posed no threat to us whatsoever (and had nothing to do with the terrorist attacks of September 11, 2001) because the corporate media and the Intelligence community told them Saddam was going to nuke Kansas City ... you might assume that all these Good Americans, ashamed at having been made fools of by a bunch of television talking heads and "papers of record" like *The New York Times* ... you might think these folks, who, after all, are not complete idiots the corporatocracy can just hoodwink over and over again using more or less the same bag of tricks ... you might naturally assume that these Good Americans would give us the benefit of the doubt this time, i.e., those of us who are challenging the narrative the corporate media has been ramming down our throats since Hillary Clinton lost the election.

But, no ... nothing of the sort. No, this time, we're not "terrorist sympathizers." We're "Putin sympathizers," "Russian operatives," or at the very least we are "useful idiots" who are helping Russia destroy democracy by "sowing discord," "disunity," "division," and other forms of dissent throughout the West.

This is the essential feature of our new and improved official narrative. The basic storyline has not changed. It's still "Democracy versus The Terrorists." The global capitalist ruling classes are simply expanding the already arbitrary and meaningless definition of "terrorism" (or rather, and more broadly, "extremism").

This is a natural, predictable progression, which the ruling classes have been preparing us for. After sixteen years of living in fear of "the terrorists" who "hate us for our freedom," we are being introduced to a new official enemy. A new, yet familiar official enemy. An official enemy all Good Americans are already pre-programmed to hate and fear.

Yes, that's right, folks, the Rooskies are back, only this time without the Communism. No, this time, their diabolical goal is the destruction of "democracy" itself! Why, exactly, the Rooskies want to destroy democracy is not entirely clear, especially as it would collapse their economy, not to mention precipitate a nuclear war that would wipe out most forms of life on the planet. But, you know, they're inscrutable, those Rooskies.

According to the experts in the corporate media, and our corporate-sponsored representatives in government (and, it goes without saying, the Intelligence community), the primary weapon the Rooskies are using to destroy democracy, and all life on Earth, is this sowing of "divisiveness" and "discord," and "distrust" of our government and corporate elites, who love us as they love their own children, and who would never try to manipulate us, or treat us like interchangeable commodities, or bankrupt us with their Ponzi schemes, or debt-enslave our families for profit, or any other horrible things like that.

This is the type of mindless hogwash Americans are being pressured to swallow, and, in fact, are swallowing, millions of them. But then, this is how propaganda works. It doesn't have to make any sense. In fact, it's usually more effective if it doesn't.

In profoundly authoritarian cultures like the contemporary United States, people tend to believe the authorities, particularly when they're all repeating the same simple message over and over. People want to believe the authorities. They want to because they've been conditioned to want to from the time they were children by their parents, teachers, political leaders, the corporate media, television, Hollywood, cultural icons, and more or less every other ideological organ of "normal society."

This is why, when it's time to whip up popular support for a war of aggression (or a war against anyone expressing dissent), all the ruling classes have to do is make up an emotionally-loaded narrative with a halfway-believable official enemy and have their "authoritative media sources" repeat it, over, and over, and over, in a thousand different iterations, each repetition reifying the others, until the narrative becomes the axiomatic "truth," which no respectable, normal person would ever even think of wanting to question.

In fact, once an official narrative has become the axiomatic "truth," it can be extremely dangerous psychologically if these "respectable persons" are confronted with evidence that demonstrates that the official narrative (or, in other words, their "reality") is based on … well, a load of horseshit, as by this time they've forgotten it is fiction, and thus genuinely believe the lies they're telling.

If you'd like to see an example of this in action, take a few minutes and watch what happens to Luke Harding, author of the book Collusion, when he is interviewed by Aaron Maté.[2] What you will witness is Harding melting down as his "collusion" narrative (i.e., the premise of his book) falls to pieces under Maté's questioning, which remains collegial and calm throughout.

2 "Where's the Collusion?" The Real News, December 23, 2017

Clearly, it had never occurred to Harding that anyone would question the Russiagate narrative, and especially not someone else in "the business," as mainstream journalists are trained to accept and parrot whatever the ruling classes tell them. When he finally realizes what is happening, (i.e., that his "reality" is melting away like your face in the mirror on a bad acid trip), he calls Maté a "collusion rejectionist," and abruptly ends the interview.

This is just the kind of thing the corporatocracy wants to eliminate, or relegate to the margins of the Internet. They can't have journalists like Aaron Maté running around punching holes in their narrative, or at least not where normal Americans can see it.

It's all fine and good to have jokers like Hannity and Alex Jones jabbering about deep state conspiracies, as normal Americans don't take them seriously, but rational journalists like Maté, if they're not going to cooperate with the official narrative, well, then they need to be censored, or algorithmically deranked, or otherwise marginalized, and the sooner the better.

Which is exactly what the corporatocracy is doing, and what they intend to continue doing until "unity," "harmony," and "trust" is restored.

And this is just the beginning, folks. If you want to get a glimpse of our dystopian future, read this recent piece in *The Atlantic*.[3] It's by Representative Will Hurd, of Texas, but it conveys the sentiments of the corporate ruling classes and their loyal servants in government, generally. I won't spoil it for you, but here's one quote:

> "To address continued Russian disinformation campaigns, we need to develop a national counter-disinformation strategy. *The strategy needs to span the entirety of government and civil society*, to enable a coordinated effort to counter the threat that influence operations pose to our democracy. *It should implement similar principles to those in the Department of Homeland Security's Strategy for Countering Violent Extremism*, with a focus on truly understanding the threat and developing ways to shut it down."

The emphasis is mine. The Orwellianism is Hurd's. The message couldn't possibly be clearer.

---

3 Hurd, Will, "Russia Is Our Adversary," The Atlantic, February 9, 2018

If you've enjoyed the Department of Homeland Security over the course of the last sixteen years, the constant low-level paranoia, the invasive searches, the body scans, the T.S.A. agents groping your kids, the cops and soldiers standing around in public places in body armor with their assault rifles in the "sling-ready" position, the N.S.A. listening in on your phone calls, and all the other features of The War on Terror ... you're going to love The War on Dissent.

Then They Came for the Globalists

March 23, 2018

Thank God for the corporate media. If it wasn't for them, and the ADL, I'd have probably never discovered that I'm a Nazi. Apparently, I've been one for quite some time ... which is weird, as I had no idea. Here I was, naively believing that I'd been writing about global capitalism and the realignment of political power and ideology in the post-Cold War world, when, really, I have just been persecuting the Jews.

I didn't think I was persecuting the Jews. But such is the insidious nature of thoughtcrime. When you're a Nazi thought criminal (as I apparently am), it doesn't matter what you think you're thinking. What matters is what the global capitalist ruling classes tell you you're thinking, which it turns out is often a lot more complicated and horrible than what you thought you were thinking.

For example, I've been thinking and writing about globalism, which most dictionaries define as "a national policy of treating the whole world as a proper sphere for political influence," or "the development of socioeconomic networks that transcend national boundaries," or something like that ... which was more or less my understanding of the term. Little did I know that these fake "definitions" had been infiltrated into these dictionaries by discord-sowing Strasserist agents to dupe political satirists like myself into unknowingly spreading anti-Semitism as part of Putin's Master Plan to destroy the United States of America and establish worldwide Nazi domination.

Fortunately, the lexicography experts in the corporate media and the Anti-Defamation League cleared that up for me earlier this month. According to these experts, words like "globalist" and "globalism" don't really mean anything. They are simply Nazi code words for "the Jews." There is actually no such thing as "globalism," or "global capitalism," or "transnational capitalism," or "supranational quasi-governmental entities" like the International Monetary Fund, the World Trade Organization, the European Commission, and the European Central Bank … or, OK, sure, there *are* such entities, but there is no legitimate reason to discuss them, or write about them, or even casually mention them, and anyone who does is definitely a Nazi.

Now, imagine my horror when I took that in, especially given my repeated references to "the corporatocracy," "global capitalism," and "the global capitalist ruling classes" in the essays I've been publishing recently. I didn't want to accept it at first, but the more "authoritative sources" I consulted, the more glaringly obvious my thoughtcrimes became.

These authoritative sources were reacting to Trump referring to Gary Cohn as "a globalist" in his rambling remarks in the Oval Office, which went a little something like this:

> "He may be a globalist, but I still like him. He is seriously a globalist. There's no question … in his own way. But you know what, he's also a nationalist. He loves our country and … where is Gary?"

While the experts are still scouring the video for Nazi gestures and facial expressions, there can be no doubt that Trump said the word "globalist." The corporate media and the ADL could not allow this transgression to stand.

Peter Beinart, writing in *The Atlantic*,[1] explained that "globalist" is "an epithet … a modern-day vessel for a slur" against the Jews, and he linked to a video of Jonathan Greenblatt, CEO of the ADL, who verified that "the term 'globalist' was developed and originated in extremist circles populated by white supremacists" (by which I can only assume he meant the anti-globalization movement, which apparently is just a big Nazi front).

Eli Rosenberg, in *The Washington Post*,[2] although allowing that "globalist" can sometimes mean "globalist," emphasized that, "to some observers of extremism," it also "speaks to something darker."

1 Beinart, Peter, "What Trump Means When He Calls Gary Cohn a 'Globalist'," The Atlantic, March 9, 2018

2 Rosenberg, Eli, "Trump and Mulvaney called Gary Cohn a 'globalist.' Is that anti-Semitic?" The Washington Post, March 9, 2018

Bret Stephens, writing in *The New York Times*,[3] couldn't quite decide whether using the word makes you an official goose-stepping Nazi or just a garden variety anti-Semite.

CNN's Don Lemon, delving into "the ugly history" of the word, explained that "it is shorthand for a worldview based on racism, xenophobia, and anti-Semitism" ... the worldview of "far right conspiracy theorists obsessed with prominent Jews like George Soros."[4]

And these are just a few of the many examples.

After processing all these authoritative statements by these respected experts and credible news sources, I felt like I'd been walking around with a Swastika branded into my forehead. I was overcome by a sudden need to signal my anti-anti-Semitism to my friends, family, and the world at large.

After destroying my old Pink Floyd CDs and apologizing to Jerry Seinfeld on Twitter,[5] I immediately ran and confessed to my wife, who just happens to be "a globalist," and begged her to call her family members who control the media, the banks, and Hollywood and ask them to forgive me my thoughtcrimes. Then I drafted an email to the SPLC asking whether they could possibly squeeze me into their interactive Hate Map somewhere, or at least get some neo-McCarthyite hack to publish a ridiculous, paranoid smear piece[6] about my Nazi vocabulary on their website.

Seriously, though, all satire aside, this stigmatization of terms like "globalist," "globalism," and "global capitalism" is a key component of The War on Dissent which the global capitalist ruling classes have been waging against a broad assortment of insurgent elements for the last eighteen months. It isn't just a question of delegitimizing dissidents by smearing them as anti-Semites, Russian agents, and

3 Stephens, Bret, "In Praise of Globalists," The New York Times, March 9, 2018

4 Schwartz, Ian, "Don Lemon: The Term 'Globalist' Is Racist, Anti-Semitic," Real Clear Politics, March 10, 2018

5 Schwartz, Yakov, "Seinfeld under fire over visit to West Bank 'military camp'," Times of Israel, January 11, 2018 (Yes, I'm afraid I mocked Jerry Seinfeld after photos of him at a West Bank "anti-terrorism" course were posted online.)

6 Flood, Brian, "Southern Poverty Law Center apologizes after painting journalists as fascists in retracted article," Fox News, March 16, 2018 ("The controversial, far-left Southern Poverty Law Center was forced to retract and apologize for an article that falsely asserted several reporters were enabling white supremacists and Russia while labeling them as fascists and racists. The SPLC on March 9 published the misleading article by Alexander Reid Ross headlined, 'The multipolar spin: how fascists operationalize left-wing resentment.'")

conspiracy theorists. The goal is also to conceal the essential nature of the conflict itself.

The essential nature of the conflict is ... neoliberalism versus neo-nationalism. This is what we are experiencing currently, not a Russian assault on Western democracy, nor even a resumption of the Cold War, but, rather, the global capitalist ruling classes putting down a neo-nationalist insurgency ... the insurgency that led to the Brexit referendum and the presidency of Donald Trump.

Now, here's where things get a little tricky, particularly for those of us on the Left (whatever that label even means anymore). The neo-nationalists can come right out and call the conflict what it is. It is in their interest to call it what it is. They may not be opposing capitalism, but they are certainly opposing *global* capitalism. In doing so, they are attracting people who are not so thrilled about being governed by unaccountable global corporations and supranational non-governmental bodies, people who are still emotionally attached to outdated concepts like national sovereignty, national culture, and crazy stuff like that. Some of these folks are actual neo-Nazis, but most of them are just regular people who know when they are being pissed on by global capitalism and told it's raining. The point is, the neo-nationalists can describe their opponents as exactly what they are, global capitalists, or just plain old globalists. Neoliberals do not have this luxury.

See, the problem for the capitalist ruling classes is that global neoliberalism (i.e., globalism) is a really tough sell to regular folks. They can't just come out and explain to people that national sovereignty is essentially dead, and that political power now resides among a network of global corporations (which couldn't care less about their "nationality") exploiting a globalized labor market (which is why their "good jobs" are not coming back) and a globalized financial market (which is why almost everything is being privatized and their families are being debt-enslaved). Nor can they admit that the "War on Terror" and the European refugee crisis it has caused, and the chaos and slaughter in Iraq, Afghanistan, Libya, Yemen, Syria, et cetera, is the predictable result of global capitalism aggressively restructuring the Greater Middle East, which it started doing more or less immediately after the collapse of the Soviet Union (i.e., as soon as the final impediment to its pursuit of global hegemony was removed). This kind of thing doesn't go over very well, not with most regular working class people.

So what the global capitalist ruling classes have to do is ... well, they have to lie. They have to disseminate a different narrative, a narrative that has nothing to do with the hegemony of global capitalism, the dissolution of national sovereignty, and the privatization of virtually everything. Because people aren't total morons, this narrative needs to bear some resemblance to the actual conflict taking place. So, all right, a little rebranding is in order. Global neoliberalism becomes "Western democracy," neo-nationalism becomes "Nazism," and Vladimir Putin becomes Adolf Hitler.

Presto! Now things are nice and simple! History, geopolitics, and socioeconomics vanish into the ether! Capitalism schmapitalism! This is no time for critical thinking, not with Putin-Nazis coming out of the woodwork! No, this is a time to rally behind the freedom fighters at the FBI, the CIA, the corporate media, and the rest of the military industrial complex, and to mercilessly hunt down Russian infiltrators, Putin sympathizers, crypto-Assadists, neo-Strasserian, alt-right entryists, and other sowers of division and discord! We need to get these folks delegitimitized, stigmatized as racists and anti-Semites, or terrorists, or some other type of "extremist," before they can "influence" anyone else with their Facebook ads and subversive essays.

You will know them by the words they use, and by the words they do not use. Anybody using words like "globalist," "global capitalism," or "neoliberal," or suggesting that anyone voted for Trump or Brexit for any reason other than racism, you can pretty much rest assured that they're Nazis. Also, anyone writing about "banks" or the "deep state." Absolutely Nazis. Oh yeah, and the "corporate media," naturally. Only Putin-Nazis talk like that. Oh, and definitely anyone who hasn't spent the last two years attacking Trump (as if there has been anything else to focus on), or has implied that "the Russians" aren't out to destroy us, or that the historical moment we are living through might be just a bit more complex than that ... well, you know what they're really saying. They're saying, "we need to exterminate the Jews."

Look, I could go on and on with this, but I don't think I really need to. Remember, I'm a Nazi thought criminal now. So just go back and read through some of my essays and make note of all the coded Nazi messages, or check with the Anti-Defamation League, or the SPLC, or the corporate media, or ... well, just ask the good folks at Google.[7]

---

7 Hopkins, C. J., "Who's Afraid of Corporate COINTELPRO," CounterPunch, November 3, 2017 ("A couple weeks ago, I googled myself, and noticed that two of my published books had disappeared from the Google 'Knowledge Panel' that appears in the upper right of the search results. I also noticed that the people 'People Also Search For' in the panel had changed. For years, consistently, the people you saw there had been a variety of other elitist literary wankers and leftist types. Suddenly, they were all rather right-wing types, people like Ilana Mercer, John Derbyshire, and other VDARE writers. So that was a little disconcerting.")

Jeremy Corbyn's Nazi Death Cult

April 6, 2018

So it appears the British are our last best hope of stemming the blood-dimmed Putin-Nazi tide that has shaken the foundations of Western democracy since Hillary Clinton lost the election. The neoliberal Resistance in the United States, led by the U.S. intelligence agencies, the Democratic Party, and the corporate media, fights on, but it's a losing battle. Despite their control of most of the press, most members of the US Congress, and the military industrial complex, they are just no match for the fearsome power of Vladimir Putin's international army of Putin-Nazi-brainwashing specialists and the evil genius of Donald Trump.

All is not lost by any means — there is still the chance that the CIA might stage a coup, or a heart attack — but for now it seems that the ruling classes (and the millions of Americans who identify with them) are lying low and biding their time like Camembert-slurping surrender monkeys.

Thus, once again, it's up to the Brits to save democracy from annihilation. They're doing a bang-up job of it so far. Just look at how they've responded to the so-called "Labour Anti-Semitism Crisis," which exploded just a few short weeks ago.

No sooner had members of the neoliberal Blairite wing of the Labour Party dug up a six-year-old Facebook post in which Jeremy Corbyn had the gall to wonder why a mural depicting a group of bankers (some of them sporting rather large schnozzes) needed to be removed from view than the British ruling classes sprang into action.

Clearly, this 2012 Facebook post was proof that the Corbyn-led Labour Party had been infiltrated by a Nazi death cult bent on brainwashing gullible leftists into "failing to recognize Anti-Semitism," using unwords like "Zionist," and inappropriately criticizing Israel.

The public needed to be alerted immediately, so the corporate media started pumping out stories repeating the words "Corbyn" and "anti-Semitism," over and over, in a variety of contexts. At this point, there have been literally hundreds of them.

The conservative press has been entirely predictable, running headlines like "Jeremy Corbyn's Hate Factory,"[1] "Once in the shadows, anti-Semitism is now entrenched at the poisoned heart of the Labour Party,"[2] "Theresa May slams Jeremy Corbyn for letting anti-Semitism, misogyny and hatred run free in Labour,"[3] and so on, but it's the liberal media that are doing the heavy lifting.

The Independent warned the world that "Labour's antisemitic cancer shows the party for what it has become — a cult of keyboard warriors and raging Corbynistas."[4] Michael Segalov, writing in *The Guardian*, put potential Corbyn-apologists on notice: "If you can't see antisemitism, it's time to open your eyes."[5] Owen Jones has been conducting a virtual one-man anti-anti-Semitism crusade, reminding the public on an hourly basis that "the poison of anti-Semitism" exists, and "the left has to get its house in order," and otherwise reinforcing the connection of Corbyn with anti-Semitism.

Which, of course, is the purpose of this manufactured "crisis," i.e., to associate Jeremy Corbyn with anti-Semitism in the public consciousness. The content of all these impassioned articles (whether attacking or defending Corbyn) is, if not irrelevant, secondary. Their primary aim is to generate the "crisis," and then position Corbyn in the middle of it.

Here's a quick lesson on how that works.

Say, for example, we wanted to simulate a "Racism Crisis" in Hollywood and smear a certain producer with it. This should be easy enough to do, as there is plenty of racism in Hollywood to work

---

1 Kerbaj, Richard and Pogrund, Gabriel, "Exposed: Jeremy Corbyn's Hate Factory," The Times, April 1, 2018

2 Littlejohn, Richard, "Once in the shadows, anti-Semitism is now entrenched at the poisoned heart of the Labour Party," Daily Mail, September 27, 2017

3 Tolhurst, Alain, "Theresa May slams Jeremy Corbyn for letting anti-Semitism, misogyny and hatred run free in Labour," The Sun, October 4, 2017

4 Peck, Tom, "Labour's antisemitic cancer shows the party for what it has become — a cult of keyboard warriors and raging Corbynistas," The Independent, April 2, 2018

5 Segalov, Michael, "If you can't see antisemitism, it's time to open your eyes," The Guardian, March 28, 2018

with (just as there is plenty of anti-Semitism in the Labour Party, and in most other major political parties). And let's say we want to kick off this "crisis" by citing some "inappropriate response" by some well-known producer to a Facebook post about a movie featuring a "Magical Negro," that loveable, mystical African-American who exists to serve the white protagonist, a familiar stock character in American cinema.

OK, so we go dig up that post, in which our target "fails to recognize the racist nature" of the Magical Negro depicted in whichever movie we choose, *Forrest Gump*, *The Shawshank Redemption*, *The Green Mile*, *The Shining*, *The Matrix*, or whatever, and we demand a full confession and apology.

Next, we go digging for any other comments, posts, tweets, quotes, or hearsay that we can easily construe as "glaring proof" of our target's unreconstructed racism. At the same time (and this is absolutely crucial), we go digging among our target's current and former associates, and their associates, and any random Facebook groups our target has ever carelessly joined, and tweets our target has ever carelessly "liked," and anything else we can possibly link to him, until we can claim to have firmly established that Hollywood is experiencing a "racism crisis," and that a "cancer of racism" is running rampant through the Screen Actors Guild and Writers Guild West.

Then we get our associates in the corporate media to make an incredibly big stink out of it, and argue "both sides" of the "crisis" we've just generated. Half the media can attack our target as a racist or a racism enabler. The other half can do the Owen Jones schtick, repeatedly confessing that, yes, indeed, Hollywood has a racism problem, a corrosive, longstanding racism problem, which has suddenly grown to crisis proportions and ... I think you get the general idea.

This is just an example, of course. Clearly, there's no racism crisis in Hollywood, or, rather, the global capitalist ruling classes have no reason to generate one. They do, however, have a reason to generate an "anti-Semitism crisis" and use it to demonize Jeremy Corbyn, and anyone else they deem an enemy.

As I've been documenting for almost two years now, the global capitalist ruling classes are putting down a nationalist insurgency ... the populist backlash against global capitalism that led to Brexit, the election of Trump, and the rise of neo-nationalist parties in Europe. They are conducting this counter-insurgency against an assortment of forces on both the left and the right. (Ideology makes no difference to capitalism, which can accommodate pretty much any ideology as long as it doesn't interfere with the market.)

Hard as it is to get our minds around, what we have been living through since 2016 is not a battle between the Left and the Right. It is a battle over national sovereignty.

Since the end of the Cold War, global capitalism has been dissolving national sovereignty and replacing it with supranational sovereignty. *Corporate* supranational sovereignty. A lot of people, on both the Left and the Right, are not real happy with how that is going, and are resisting the only way they know how to, by reasserting their national sovereignty. The global capitalist ruling classes cannot allow this rebellion to continue, not when it leads to events like Brexit, the election of Trump, and the destabilization of the entire Western neoliberal order.

Which brings us back to the Putin-Nazis and the War on Dissent that the global capitalist ruling classes are currently waging against any and all resistance to their brave new global capitalist world. Because they are unable to characterize the nature of this conflict as what it is, they need a convincing "official enemy" to scare the living bejesus out of people. This is where the Putin-Nazis come in.

For the last two years, as you've probably noticed, the corporate media have been not so subtly alternating between manufacturing Russia hysteria and Nazi hysteria, and sometimes whipping up both at once. Thus, I've dubbed the new Official Enemy of Freedom "the Putin-Nazis." They don't really make any sense, rationally, but let's not get all hung up on that. Official enemies don't have to make sense. The important thing is, they're coming to get us, and to kill the Jews and destroy democracy ... and something about Stalin, if memory serves. Putin is their leader, of course. Trump is his diabolical puppet. Julian Assange is ... well, Goebbels, or something. Glenn Greenwald is also on the payroll, as are countless "useful idiots" like myself, whose job it is to sow division, discord, racism, anti-Semitism, anti-capitalism, anti-Hillaryism, collusion rejectionism, ontological skepticism, and any other horrible thing you can think of.

Where does Corbyn fit into all this? Well, obviously, he's been quietly building his extreme-left Putin-Nazi Death Cult in the shadows of British politics for years. If the Blairites hadn't tracked down that telltale comment in his six-year-old Facebook post, who knows what horrors he and his legions of cultists might have unleashed on Britain.

Luckily, we won't have to find that out, because the ruling classes and the corporate media are united against the Putin-Nazi threat. They shall not flag. They shall go on to the end. They shall fight these devils in the streets and the fields, and on the hills, and on the seas and oceans. They shall defend global capitalism, whatever the cost, no matter who they have to smear as an "anti-Semite" or a "Russian agent." They shall smear them on television and on the Internet. They shall smear them in their "respectable" papers, until, in God's good time, the New World, with all its corporate power and might, steps forth to the liberation of the old ...

Oh, gosh, here I am, over my word limit, and I got all wrapped up in that Churchill parody and completely forgot to virtuously signal my steadfast opposition to anti-Semitism.

But then I've never been very good at responding to emotionally manipulative Pavlovian stimuli.

I'll have to work a little harder on that.

The Simulation of Democracy

May 23, 2018

One of the most complicated and frustrating aspects of operating a global capitalist empire is maintaining the fiction that it doesn't exist. Virtually every action you take has to be carefully recontextualized or otherwise spun for public consumption. Every time you want to bomb or invade some country to further your interests, you have to mount a whole public relations campaign. You can't even appoint a sadistic torture freak to run your own coup-fomenting agency,[1] or shoot a few thousand unarmed people you've imprisoned in a de facto ghetto,[2] without having to do a big song and dance about "defending democracy" and "democratic values."

Naked despotism is so much simpler, not to mention more emotionally gratifying. Ruling an empire as a godlike dictator means never having to say you're sorry. You can torture and kill anyone you want, and conquer and exploit whichever countries you want, without having to explain yourself to anyone. Also, you get to have your humongous likeness muraled onto the walls of buildings, make people swear allegiance to you, and all that other cool dictator stuff.

Global capitalists do not have this luxury.

Generating the simulation of democracy that most Western consumers desperately need in order to be able to pretend to believe that they are not just smoothly-functioning cogs in the machinery of a murderous global empire managed by a class of obscenely wealthy and powerful international elites to whom their lives mean exactly nothing, although extremely expensive and time-consuming, is essential to maintaining their monopoly on power. Having condi-

---

1 Smith, David, "Torture allegations dog Gina Haspel as she is poised to be first female CIA head," The Guardian, March 16, 2018

2 Kubovich, Yaniv and Khoury, Jack, "15 Killed, Dozens Wounded as Thousands Gather on Israel-Gaza Border," Haaretz, April 28, 2019

tioned most Westerners into believing they are "free," and not just glorified peasants with gadgets, the global capitalist ruling classes have no choice but to keep up this fiction. Without it, their empire would fall apart at the seams.

This is the devil's bargain modern capitalism made back in the 18th Century. In order to wrest power from the feudal aristocracies that had dominated the West throughout the Middle Ages, the bourgeoisie needed to sell the concept of "democracy" to the unwashed masses, who they needed both to staff their factories and, in some cases, to fight revolutionary wars, or depose and publicly guillotine monarchs. All that gobbledegook about taxes, tariffs, and the unwieldy structure of the feudal system was not the easiest sell to the peasantry. "Liberty" and "equality" went over much better. So "democracy" became their rallying cry, and, eventually, the official narrative of capitalism. The global capitalist ruling classes have been stuck with "democracy" ever since, or, more accurately, with the simulation of democracy.

The purpose of this simulation of democracy is not to generate fake democracy and pass it off as real democracy. Its purpose is to generate the *concept* of democracy, the only form in which democracy exists. It does this by casting a magic spell (which I'll do my best to demystify in a moment) that deceives us into perceiving the capitalist marketplace we Westerners inhabit, not as a market, but as a society. An essentially democratic society. Not a fully fledged democratic society, but a society progressing toward "democracy" … which it is, and simultaneously isn't.

Obviously, life under global capitalism is more democratic than under feudal despotism, not to mention more comfortable and entertaining. Capitalism isn't "evil" or "bad." It's a machine. Its fundamental function is to eliminate any and all despotic values and replace them with a single value, i.e., exchange value, determined by the market.

This despotic-value-decoding machine is what freed us from the tyranny of kings and priests, which it did by subjecting us to the tyranny of capitalists and the meaningless value of the so-called free market, wherein everything is just another commodity … toothpaste, cell phones, healthcare, food, education, cosmetics, et cetera.

Despite that, only an idiot would argue that capitalism is not preferable to despotism, or that it hasn't increased our measure of freedom. So, yes, we have evolved toward democracy, if we're comparing modern capitalism to medieval feudalism.

The problem is that capitalism is never going to lead to *actual* democracy (i.e., government by and for the people). This is never going to happen.

In fact, capitalism has already reached the limits of the freedom it can safely offer us. This freedom grants us the ability to make an ever-expanding variety of choices, none of which have much to do with democracy. For example, Western consumers are free to work for whatever corporation they want, and to buy whatever products they want, and to assume as much debt as the market will allow to purchase a home wherever they want, and to worship whichever gods they want (as long as they conform their behavior to the values of capitalism and not their religion), and men can transform themselves into women, and white people can deem themselves African Americans, or Native Americans, or whatever they want, and anyone can mock or insult the President or the Queen of England on Facebook and Twitter … none of which freedoms were even imaginable, much less possible, under feudal despotism.

But this is as far as our "freedom" goes. The global capitalist ruling classes are never going to allow us to govern ourselves, not in any meaningful way.

In fact, since the mid-1970s, they've been systematically dismantling the framework of social democracy throughout the West, and otherwise relentlessly privatizing everything. They've been doing this more slowly in Europe, where social democracy is more entrenched, but, make no mistake, American "society" is the model for our dystopian future. The ruling classes and their debt-enslaved servants, protected from the desperate masses by squads of hyper-militarized police, medicated in their sanitized enclaves, watching Westworld on Amazon Prime as their shares in private prisons rise and the forces of democracy defend their freedom by slaughtering men, women, and children in some faraway country they can't find on a map, and would never visit on vacation anyway … this is where the USA already is, and where the rest of the West is headed.

Which is why it is absolutely crucial to maintain the simulation of democracy, and the fiction that we're still living in a world where major geopolitical events are determined by sovereign nations and their leaders, rather than by global corporations and a class of supranational elites whose primary allegiance is to global capitalism, rather than to any specific nation, much less to the actual people who live there.

The global capitalist ruling classes need the masses in the West to believe that they live in the United States of America, the United Kingdom, Germany, France, and so on, and not in a global marketplace. Because, if it's all one global marketplace, with one big global labor force (which global corporations can exploit with impunity), and if it's one big global financial system (where the economies of supposed adversaries like China and the United States, or the European Union and Russia, are almost totally interdependent), then there is no United States of America, no United Kingdom, no France, no Germany ... or not as we're conditioned to perceive them. There is only the global capitalist empire, divided into "national" market territories, each performing slightly different administrative functions within the empire ... and those territories that have not yet surrendered their sovereignty and been absorbed into it.

I think you know which those territories are.

But getting back to the simulation of democracy (the purpose of which is to prevent us from perceiving the world as I just suggested above), how that works is, we are all conditioned to believe we are living in these imperfect democracies, which are inexorably evolving toward "real" democracy but just haven't managed to get there quite yet. "Real" being the key word here, because there is no such thing as real democracy. There never has been, except among relatively small and homogenous groups of people. Like Baudrillard's Disneyland, "Western democracy" is presented to us as "imperfect" or "unfinished" (in other words, as a replica of "real democracy") in order to convince us that there exists such a thing as "real democracy," which we will achieve ... someday.

This is how simulations work. The replica does not exist to deceive us into believing that it is the "real" thing. It exists to convince us that there *is* a "real" thing. In essence, it invokes the "real" thing by pretending to be a copy of it. Just as the images of God in church invoke the "god" of which they are copies (if only in the minds of the faithful), our imperfect replica of democracy invokes the concept of "real democracy" (which does not exist, and has never existed, beyond the level of tribes and bands).

This is, of course, ceremonial magic … but then so is everything else, really. Take out a twenty dollar bill, or a twenty Euro note, or your driver's license. They are utterly valueless, except as symbols, but no less powerful for being just symbols.

Or look at some supposedly solid object under an electron microscope. Try this with a tablespoon. As that bald kid in *The Matrix* put it, you will "realize that there is no spoon," or, rather, that there is only the spoon we've created by believing there is a spoon.

Look, I don't mean to get all spooky. What that kid (among various others throughout history) was trying to get us to understand is that we create "reality," collectively, with symbols … or we allow a "reality" to be created for us.

Our collective "reality" is also our religion, in that we live our lives and raise our children according to its precepts and values, regardless of whatever other rituals we may or may not engage in on the weekend. Western consumers, no matter whether nominally Christians, Jews, Muslims, atheists, or of any other faith, live their lives and raise their children according to the values and rules of capitalism.

Capitalism is our religion. Like every religion, it has a cosmology.

In the cosmology of global capitalism, "democracy" is capitalist heaven. We hear it preached about throughout our lives, we're surrounded by graven images of it, but we don't get to see it until we're dead.

Attempting to storm its pearly gates, or to create the Kingdom of Democracy on Earth, is heresy, and is punishable by death. Denying its existence is blasphemy, for which the punishment is excommunication, and consignment to the City of Dis, where the lost souls shout back and forth at each other across the lower depths of the Internet, their infernal voices unheard by the faithful … but, hey, don't take the word of an apostate like me. Go ahead, try it, and see what happens.

Awaiting the Putin-Nazi Apocalypse

June 15, 2018

I don't know about you, but I'm getting a little tired of waiting for the Hitlerian nightmare that the corporate media promised us was coming back in 2016. Frankly, I'm beginning to suspect that all their apocalyptic pronouncements were just part of some elaborate cocktease. I mean, here we are, a year and half into the reign of the Trumpian Reich, and ... well, where are all the concentration camps, the SS units with their death's head insignia, the Riefenstahlian parades and rallies? Trump hasn't even banned the Democratic Party, or annexed Canada, or invaded Mexico, or made anybody wear color-coded armbands. If he doesn't start Hitlering relatively soon, the oracles of the corporate media are going to have some serious explaining to do.

I don't think I'm overreacting. After all, back in 2016, *The Guardian* promised us an "age of darkness,"[1] the end of "civilized order" as we know it. "Globalization is dead, and white supremacy has triumphed,"[2] one of its more hysterical pundits proclaimed.

"Donald Trump is actually a fascist," Michael Kinsley assured us in *The Washington Post*.[3]

Charles M. Blow of *The New York Times* warned that Trump's election was "the beginning of the end," the descent of the republic into "racial Orwellianism," whatever that's supposed to mean.[4]

Thomas Friedman called it "a moral 911."[5]

---

1 Freedland, Jonathan, "If Donald Trump wins, it'll be a new age of darkness," The Guardian, November 4, 2016

2 Mason, Paul, "Globalisation is dead, and white supremacy has triumphed," The Guardian, November 9, 2016

3 Kinsley, Michael, "Donald Trump is actually a fascist," Washington Post, December 9, 2016

4 Blow, Charles M., "Trump: Making America White Again," The New York Times, November 21, 2016

5 Schwartz, Ian, "Thomas Friedman: Trump Presidency A 'Moral 9/11,'" November 12, 2016

Paul Krugman predicted nothing short of "a global recession with no end in sight."[6]

Jonathan Chait, after heroically vowing not to flee the country with his terrified family, but to stay and fight to the bitter end, guaranteed us that the "monster," Trump, would "shake the republic to its foundations."[7]

Perhaps my seismometer is on the fritz, but I haven't detected much foundation shaking. Yes, Trump repulses me, personally. I do not like the man. I never have. I lived in New York City for fifteen years, in the 1990s and early 2000s, before he became a game show host, when he was still just a shady real estate mogul with alleged ties to organized crime[8] who occasionally appeared on Wrestlemania and just generally went about the city making a narcissistic ass of himself and plastering his gold-plated name onto everything. So I have no illusions about his character ... the man is an inveterate snake oil salesman with the moral compass of a Tijuana pimp.

All I'm saying is, we were promised Hitler, or Mussolini at the very least, and it seems like all we're getting so far is just regular old narcissistic Donald Trump.

Of course, he could just be laying low and holding back on the Hitler stuff as part of the evil master plan personally developed by Vladimir Putin to systematically brainwash Americans (with state-of-the-art mind-control Facebook ads) into embracing all-out National Socialism and marching through the streets in full Nazi regalia singing Amerika Über Alles ... at which point Trump will rip off his mask, reveal his true Hitlerian face, Steve Bannon will suddenly reappear in the turret of an M1 Abrams tank at the head of a division of rebel infantry flying giant Confederate flags as they hideously rumble down Pennsylvania Avenue, and the Putin-Nazi Holocaust will begin.

Or maybe the extremely serious, Pulitzer Prize-winning political pundit David Leonhardt is onto something.

---

6 Cancryn, Adam, "Paul Krugman: Trump will bring global recession," Politico, November 9, 2016

7 Chait, Jonathan, "Forget Canada. Stay and Fight for American Democracy," New York Magazine, November 9, 2016

8 Johnston, David Cay, "Just What Were Donald Trump's Ties to the Mob?" Politico, May 22, 2016

In a prominent op-ed in *The New York Times*,[9] Leonhardt wonders if Putin's "secret plan" is for Trump to destroy "the Atlantic alliance" by arriving late for the G7 meeting and "picking fights over artificial issues," not to mention insulting the Canadian prime minister, which, it doesn't get much more hair-raising than that.

OK, I know you're probably thinking that sounds like the hopelessly paranoid jabber of some conspiracy theorist nut on YouTube, but we're talking *The New York Times* here, folks, and a bona fide "respectable pundit" who wrote a whole 15,000-word e-book and has been interviewed by Stephen Colbert, among his many other distinguished accomplishments.

Examined in the context of other blatantly loony theories the corporate media are currently attempting to ram down our throats, Leonhardt's theory kind of makes sense.

The Guardian, another very serious newspaper, in addition to covering the repercussions of its coverage of Corbyn's Nazi Death Cult, is hot on the trail of the soon-to-be-infamous Putin-Banks-Brexit Connection.[10] According to "documents seen by *The Observer*," a *Guardian* sister publication, Arron Banks, a "Brexit bankroller," allegedly had brunch with the Russian ambassador three times instead of just once, as he had claimed![11] He was also allegedly offered a piece of some shady gold deal in exchange for the number of someone on Trump's transition team, which for some reason it was otherwise impossible to obtain.

Or whatever. It doesn't really matter what happened. The point is, Putin orchestrated Brexit, presumably as part of his secret plan to destabilize the Atlantic alliance, and then blackmailed Trump into running for president with that "pee-tape" the Democrats paid a former British spook to allege exists.

Paul Krugman of *The New York Times* concurs. In his latest extremely serious piece of totally respectable grown-up opinionating, he once again calls Trump "a quisling" (he's developed a fondness for

9 Leonhardt, David, "Trump Tries to Destroy the West," The New York Times, June 10, 2018

10 Cadwalladr, Carole and Jukes, Peter, "Arron Banks 'met Russian officials multiple times before Brexit vote'," The Guardian, June 9, 2018

11 Sabbagh, Dan and Booth, Robert, "MPs call for police to investigate Arron Banks' links to Russia," The Guardian, June 10, 2018

this term, which goes over well with *New York Times* readers) and reiterates that Trump is "a de facto foreign agent" and that "America as we know it is finished."[12]

Tragically, according to Krugman, the FBI, CIA, and other guardians of Western Democracy are utterly powerless to deal with this quisling, and his evil puppet master, Putin, because it turns out the entire Republican Party is "hopelessly, irredeemably corrupt." That's right, it appears the only chance we have to save the world from Trumpzilla and imminent Putin-Nazi Holocaust is to elect a buttload of Democrats to office, and eventually an Obama-like Democratic President, so they can launch an all-out thermonuclear war against Russia and North Korea … that'll teach these Putin-Nazis to screw around with our trade agreements!

Oh, and also, we need to cancel Brexit, and do away with all these "populist" movements that Putin has fomented all over Europe!

For example, according to billionaire George Soros, the refugee-hating League in Italy is probably another Putin-backed front, part of his scheme to "dominate the West."[13] One can only assume that the AfD, the FPÖ, Rassemblement National, and every other extreme-right party exploiting people's rage and fear in Europe are parts of Putin's grand conspiracy (except, of course, for the Ukrainian Nazis that the Western alliance put into power[14]). Soros, like billionaire Bruce Wayne before him, tired of waiting for the West to strike back, is taking matters into his own hands. Not only has he been tirelessly laboring to prevent Donald Trump from "destroying the world,"[15] now he's financing "Best for Britain," a campaign to de-brainwash the British people, who, obviously, only voted for Brexit because they'd been brainwashed by the Putin-Nazis.

I could go on and on with this. Have you heard the the one about the Putin-Nazis conspiring with the NRA?[16] How about the one

---

12 Krugman, Paul, "A Quisling and His Enablers," The New York Times, June 11, 2018

13 Squires, Nick, "Italy's hard-Right League party angrily dismisses suggestions it is funded by Kremlin," The Telegraph, June 4, 2018

14 Cohen, Stephen, "America's Collusion With Neo-Nazis," The Nation, May 2, 2018

15 Kranish, Michael "'I Must Be Doing Something Right': Billionaire George Soros Faces Renewed Attacks With Defiance," Washington Post, June 9, 2018

16 Stone, Peter and Gordon, Greg, "Web of elite Russians met with NRA execs during 2016 campaign," McClatchy DC, June 11, 2018

where Emmanuel Macron, in order to protect the French from "fake news," and division-sowing Putin-Nazi memes, wants the authority to censor the Internet?[17] Or have you read the column in which David Brooks, without a detectable trace of irony, laments the passing of international relationships "based on friendship, shared values, loyalty, and affection"[18] ... seriously, he used the word "affection" in reference to the Western alliance, one of the most ruthless, mass-murdering empires in the history of ruthless, mass-murdering empires? Oh, yeah, and I almost forgot ... MSNBC's Rachel Maddow is reporting that the North Korea summit was also orchestrated by Putin![19]

I'm not sure how much more bizarre things can get. This level of bull-goose-loony paranoia, media-generated mass hysteria, and mindless conformity would be hysterically funny if it weren't so absolutely horrifying in terms of what it says about millions of Westerners, who are apparently prepared to believe almost anything the authorities tell them, no matter how nuts.

That famous Voltaire quote comes to mind: "Those who can make you believe absurdities, can make you commit atrocities," he wrote.

Another, more disturbing way of looking at it is, people willing to believe absurdities, to switch off their critical thinking faculties in order to conform to an official narrative as blatantly ridiculous as the Putin-Nazi narrative, are people who have already surrendered their autonomy, who have traded it for the comfort of the herd. Such people cannot be reasoned with, because there isn't really anyone in there. There is only whatever mindless jabber got injected into their brain that day, the dutiful repetition of which guarantees they remain a "normal" person (who believes what other normal persons believe), and not some sort of "radical" or "extremist."

These people are the people who worry me. These normal people who, completely calmly, as if what they're saying wasn't batshit crazy,

---

17 Lantier, Alex, "Anti-'fake news' bill gives French state unchecked Internet censorship powers," World Socialist Website, June 8, 2018

18 Brooks, David, "Donald Trump is Not Playing by Your Rules," The New York Times, June 11, 2018

19 The Rachel Maddow Show, MSNBC, June 12, 2018 ("It's the one crossing on that border between North Korea and that third country. If you take that train, which doesn't come very often ... where you end up in is Russia!")

explain how Trump is just like Hitler, and how Putin is trying to take over the world. I sit there and listen and smile at these people, some of whom are friends and colleagues, people who I genuinely like, and who genuinely like me in return, but who, under the right set of circumstances, would stand by and watch me marched into prison, or worse, and not utter a word in protest.

Hardcore Hitler on Hitler in Helsinki

July 10, 2018

Here it comes, the moment we've been waiting for, when Trump and Putin meet in Helsinki to officially launch the Destruction of Democracy, and very possibly the Apocalypse itself.

That's right, folks, once again, it appears we're looking at the end of everything, because according to the corporate media, on July 16, 2018, Trump is probably going to disband NATO[1] so that Putin can invade the Baltic states, then Germany, then the rest of Europe, and then presumably order an all-out thermonuclear strike on the United States, which will pretty much end civilization as we know it.

Or perhaps the plan is to do away with NATO, withdraw all American troops from Poland,[2] let Putin rape and pillage Western Europe, and then have North Korea nuke both coasts of the US mainland (and Canada, of course) so that a Putin-Nazified Middle Amerika will have carte blanche to exterminate the Mexicans and make women wear those "Handmaid" costumes … or some other ridiculously paranoid scenario, possibly involving Susan Sarandon as some kind of Putin-Nazi triple agent.

Tragically, the neoliberal establishment is completely powerless to stop Trump and Putin from carrying out this evil scheme (whatever it turns out to be in the end), because even the US Intelligence Community has to obey the law, after all, and not do anything sneaky, or unethical, not even with the fate of democracy at stake. No, unlike the Russians, who go around blatantly poisoning people with novichok oatmeal[3] more or less whenever they like, the global capitalist

---

1 The Editorial Board, "Trump and Putin's Too-Friendly Summit," The New York Times, June 28, 2018

2 Ghitis, Frida, "Trump and Putin are meeting. What could possibly go wrong?" CNN, June 27, 2018

3 Dodd, Vikram and Morris, Steven, "Wiltshire novichok poisoning investigated by UK counter-terror police," The Guardian, July 5, 2018

ruling classes' hands are tied by their own integrity. All they can do is watch in horror as these two Hitlerian megalomaniacs destroy their entire global capitalist empire and establish a thousand-year Putin-Nazi Reich.

Thank God at least the corporate media are raising their collective voices in protest. In a recent piece in *The Washington Post*, Max Bergmann of the Center for American Progress warns that "this is a summit about appeasement, and we should be terrified that Trump is going to sell out America and its allies."[4] According to Bergmann, Trump might "accidentally" share state secrets with Putin, or promise to reduce support for our freedom-loving Ukrainian Nazis, or stop trying to overthrow the Syrian government so that Syria, with the help of Russia and Iran, can launch a sneak attack on Israel and drive "the Jews" into the sea. Worse still, Bergmann speculates, he might make "secret agreements" with Putin without telling the editors of *The Washington Post*, which … God help us all if that ever happened.

Not to be out-apocalypsed by *The Post*, Roger Cohen of *The New York Times* published a full-blown dystopian epic in which Trump, Putin, Marine Le Pen, the AfD, and an a variety of other globalist-hating Hitler-alikes establish "the Alliance of Authoritarian and Reactionary States" (the "AARS"), disband the European Union and NATO, impose international martial law, and start ethnically cleansing the West of immigrants.[5]

Matteo Salvini and Horst Seehofer, decked out in full Putin-Nazi regalia, personally supervise the genocidal purges, which frightened Europeans come to support after Putin's irresistible "fake news" bots brainwash them into believing that a little Russian girl named "Tatiana" has been abducted by Moroccan migrants off a beach along the Costa del Sol.

And as if that wasn't horrifying enough to whip folks up into a mindless frenzy, *The New York Times* (which, let's remember, is an extremely distinguished and respected newspaper, and not at all a cheap propaganda rag) produced this charming little animated film

---

4 Bergmann, Max, "The Trump-Putin summit should set off alarm bells," Washington Post, June 28, 2018

5 Cohen, Roger, "Of Course It Could Not Happen Here," The New York Times, June 29, 2018

depicting Putin and Trump as ... well, a couple of tongue-sucking, titty-pinching homos.[6]

I found this kind of odd at first, as I had thought such ugly anti-gay sentiment had disappeared from liberal society, but apparently it's fine in Resistance circles to stigmatize your enemies as butt-humping queers in order to render them more repulsive in the eyes of your sophisticated, liberal audience. I did a little research, and it appears this "Hitler on Hitler" porno the *Times* produced is just the latest in a rather long line of Trump-on-Putin "homo" jokes, which are perfectly harmless when told by liberals, but when told by conservatives are homophobic hate crimes.[7]

Look, I'm not a fan of poofter humor, or the corporate media, or the so-called "Resistance," but neither am I a fan of Trump, nor am I, technically, an employee of Putin. What I am is a student of propaganda, media manipulation, and mass hysteria, and though I experienced the roll-out of the War on Terror, and assorted other propaganda campaigns (like Obama's "Hope and Change" routine, Reagan's "Morning in America" schtick, George H.W. Bush's "New World Order," and Bill Clinton's "Third Way" happy horseshit), I have never witnessed anything like this.

Most of those other propaganda campaigns at least bore some vague resemblance to reality. What we're experiencing now is more akin to the kind of behavior that goes on in cults, where people are conditioned to surrender their reason (and, ultimately, to conform their perception itself) to whatever paranoid official narrative the leader of the cult has invented, and eventually to direct their fear and hatred, not only at the cult's official enemy, but at anyone who questions the cult's "reality."

If you believe cults work because people are gullible, or stupid, you need to do some research. Cults work because their members are gradually conditioned to detach from "society" (i.e., the social body

---

6 "Trump and Putin – A Love Story," one of a series of three short video cartoons that combine real Donald Trump audio clips with hand-drawn fantasy animations by Bill Plympton, produced by Billy Shebar and David Roberts of 110th Street Films (video available online at https://110th-street.com)

7 Stern, Marlow, "Bill Maher One-Ups Colbert, Airs Fake Photo of Trump Performing Oral Sex on Putin," Daily Beast, August 12, 2017 (Hilarious coverage of Stephen Colbert referring to Trump as "Putin's cock holster," and featuring a Bill Maher meme of Trump performing fellatio on Putin in a canoe.)

that conditioned them as children) and conform to the social body of the cult. This conditioning happens systematically, often over the course of years. Scientology cult members are not introduced to the "body thetans" story the day they walk in. Nor were the Manson girls ready to butcher a house full of people for Charlie at first. It took months of orgies, acid trips, and other de- and re-programming techniques to get them to buy into his paranoid prophecy of Imminent Racist Hippie Apocalypse.

Which is what I find so disturbing, presently. The ease with which the neoliberal ruling classes have programmed millions of Western consumers to believe a narrative no less ridiculous than Scientology's "body thetans," Manson's "Helter Skelter" ... or take your pick of any number of other cult narratives.

The speed at which they switched from the War on Terror narrative to the Putin-Nazi narrative attests to the power of the corporate media and the neoliberal propaganda machine, generally. It really is an amazing achievement. In less than two years, they have managed to condition a significant portion of the Western masses to forget about the "Islamic terrorists" that they had been conditioned to live in fear of, and to transfer their fear and hatred to Trump, and Putin, and anyone who appears to support them, or doesn't sufficiently hate and fear them.

The ruling classes have achieved this feat by generating an ongoing series of episodes of mass hysteria. Most of them last a week or two, but their cumulative effect is powerful and enduring. Fake news, bots, travel bans, Confederate statues, neo-Nazi rallies, "novichok" attacks, kids in cages ... anything the corporate media can use to channel more hatred toward Trump and Putin.

None of these episodes are generated out of whole cloth. Obviously, the Russians *are* pursuing their interests, there *is* a white supremacist subculture in the U.S.A. (as there always has been), those kids *were* put in those cages, and so on ... none of which began with Trump, or has anything exclusively to do with Putin, or triggered mass protests and widespread outrage until the neoliberal ruling classes and corporate media decided it should.

The upcoming summit is next on the list. It won't be as juicy as the baby concentration camps, but it will do as far as reminding people that Trump is a secret Russian operative, or traitor (or quisling, as Paul Krugman would have it), conspiring with Putin to destroy democracy ... that is, when they're not fellating each other.

Once the summit has come and gone, and democracy has miraculously survived, they will generate another round of Hitler hysteria, and Resistance cultists will spring into action like salivating Pavlov's dogs, denouncing whatever unspeakable horror they had completely ignored for the previous eight years, jabbering about concentration camps, and ripping MAGA baseball caps off teenagers. Purely for the sake of entertainment, I'm hoping it will be the secret Nazi code the Department of Homeland Security is embedding in its press materials,[8] presumably to alert the Underground Network of Putin-Nazi Militias to stand by for imminent government takeover, the "securing of the future for white people and their children," and the weeks of homosexual Odinist orgies that are sure to follow.

Seriously, though, the absolute genius of the ruling classes' Putin-Nazi narrative (which rational people are underestimating) is that it is virtually impossible to criticize it without being labeled a Trump supporter, a Putin apologist, or a crypto-Nazi.

Like Scientology's Suppressive Persons (i.e., those who criticize Scientology), these Putin-Nazi narrative deniers "seek to upset, continuously undermine, spread bad news about and denigrate" the cult. These are typically ex-cult members who no longer subscribe to the official cult teachings, and are thus an existential ideological threat. Such persons are to be stigmatized and shunned, "so that others will know not to associate with them." (Those quotes are from the Scientology website, but the same rules apply in every cult.)

Glenn Greenwald is probably the best example of a prominent Putin-Nazi narrative denier (and he is harassed for it on an daily basis), but an hour or two of research on Twitter will reveal the same dynamic at work against much less famous "pillow biting traitors."

Nor is it just fanatical cultists on Twitter. No, if you happened to google your humble narrator at any point during the last nine months, and were concerned that the people "People Also Search For" in my Google "Knowledge Panel" were mostly "alt-right" types

8 Kushner, Aviya, "Are '14' And '88' Nazi Dog Whistles In Border Security Document — Or Just Numbers?" Forward, June 28, 2018

... well, I wrote about that in November of last year.[9] I have since repeatedly written to Google and suggested they should occasionally alternate the anti-Semites they are associating me with, as using the exactly the same ones for months is lazy, and makes it extremely difficult to blame their "search results" on some innocent algorithm.

But what do I know? Maybe I'm just paranoid, and Google isn't out to get me. Or maybe they know me better than myself, and I really am a crypto-Nazi, or some other kind of Suppressive Person, and democracy really is on the brink of disaster.

After all, Glenn Greenwald just flew over to Moscow, and was selfied in the company of Edward Snowden, and Putin is poisoning random people in Amesbury for no apparent reason,[10] and Susan Sarandon hacked the election,[11] or dropped a Sarin bomb on Douma, or else Putin did, or maybe it was Xenu, or the Russians are about to take down the entire American fiber-optic network,[12] and I almost forgot those four hundred white supremacist idiots who are planning to gather and bellow Nazi slogans at each other in Lafayette Square on August 12, and who are already receiving international coverage,[13] because we can't afford to ignore a few hundred racist morons in polo shirts ... if we did, well, who knows what that might lead to?

People might actually have a moment to pause and think about what's going on, and why it's going on, and who it serves, and try to put it all into some kind of perspective, before they react to the next Pavlovian stimulus the media waves in their faces.

Ready? Good. Because here it comes ...

---

9 Hopkins, C. J. "Who's Afraid of Corporate COINTELPRO?" CounterPunch, November 3, 2017

10 Wall, Tom, "Novichok fear sends chill through Salisbury's homeless," The Observer, July 8, 2018

11 Hyde, Marina, "Protest all you like, Susan Sarandon. In effect you work for Trump," The Guardian, July 5, 2018

12 MSN, among numerous other corporate media outlets, suggested this scenario as part of their pre-release promotion of Active Measures, a 2018 film by Jack Bryan. According to Wikipedia, this was "the first major documentary to address the allegations of 'collusion' between the Trump campaign and agents of the Russian state." The MSN video has since been removed from the Internet.

13 Lennard, Natasha, "A Year Later, the Fascists of Charlottesville Are Back for More — This Time Outside the White House," The Intercept, July 2, 2018

Trump's Treasonous Traitor Summit, or: How Liberals Learned to Stop Worrying and Love the New McCarthyism

July 18, 2018

So it appears America and democracy have miraculously survived the dreaded Trump-Putin summit, or Trump's meeting with his Russian handler, as the neoliberal ruling classes and their mouthpieces in the corporate media would dearly like us all to believe. NATO has not been summarily dissolved. Poland has not been invaded by Russia. The offices of *The New York Times*, *The Washington Post*, CNN, and MSNBC have not been stormed by squads of jackbooted Trumpian Gestapo. The Destabilization of the Middle East, the Privatization of Virtually Everything, the Conversion of the Planet into One Big Shopping Mall, and other global capitalist projects are all going forward uninterrupted. Apart from Trump making a narcissistic, word-salad-babbling jackass of himself, which he does on a more or less daily basis, nothing particularly apocalyptic happened.

And so, once again, Western liberals, and others obsessed with Donald Trump, having been teased into a painfully tumescent paroxysm of anticipation of some unimaginably horrible event that would finally lead to Trump's impeachment (or his removal from office by other means) were left standing around with their hysteria in their hands. It has become a sadistic ritual at this point … like a twisted, pseudo-Tantric exercise where the media get liberals all lathered up over whatever fresh horror Trump has just perpetrated (or some non-story story they have invented out of whole cloth), build the tension for several days, until liberals are moaning and begging for impeachment, or a full-blown CIA-sponsored coup, then pull out abruptly and leave the poor bastards writhing in agony until the next time ... which is pretty much exactly what just happened.

In the days and weeks leading up to the summit, the Resistance deployed every weapon in its arsenal to whip the Western masses up into a frenzy of anti-Putin-Nazi fervor. While continuing to flog the wildly popular baby concentration camp story[1] (because the Hitler stimulus never fails to elicit a Pavlovian response from Americans, regardless of how often or how blatantly you use it), the corporate media began hammering hard on the "Trump is a Russian Agent" hysteria. (Normally, the corporate media alternates between the Hitler hysteria and the Russia hysteria so as not to completely short-circuit the already scrambled brains of Western liberals, but given the imminent threat of a peace deal,[2] they needed to go the whole hog this time and paint this summit as a secret, internationally televised assignation between Hitler and ... well, Hitler).

In order to render them even more repugnant in the eyes of Western liberals (as if being two Hitlers wasn't repugnant enough), *The New York Times* produced a short porno graphically depicting Trump and Putin as insatiably horny homosexual lovers.[3]

A fusillade of apocalyptic op-eds followed, the most shamelessly paranoid and hysterical of which was Roger Cohen's experimental dystopia, in which "The Alliance of Authoritarian and Reactionary States" trick the inherently fascist Europeans into launching a Second Holocaust with a "fake news" story about Moroccan migrants abducting poor little "Tatiana" from a beach resort in Fuengirola.[4]

While faithful *New York Times*-reading liberals were still struggling to regain control of their sphincters and doubling up on their

1 Pitzer, Andrea, "Trump's tent city for children is a concentration camp," San Francisco Chronicle, June 21, 2018

2 Coates, Sam and Waterfield, Bruno, "Fears grow over prospect of Trump 'peace deal' with Putin," The Times, June 28, 2018

3 "Trump and Putin - A Love Story," one of a series of three short video cartoons that combine real Donald Trump audio clips with hand-drawn fantasy animations by Bill Plympton, produced by Billy Shebar and David Roberts of 110th Street Films (video available online at https://110th-street.com)

4 Cohen, Roger, "Of Course It Could Not Happen Here," The New York Times, June 29, 2018

Alprazolam prescriptions in a desperate attempt to banish these visions of the coming butch-gay Putin-Nazi Reich, go-to propagandist, Jonathan Chait, who has obviously been watching way too much *Homeland*, published a paranoid spec-fic novella[5] (complete with a "Carrie is off her meds" flow chart) about how Trump has probably been "a Russian intelligence asset" since 1987.

At the same time, MSNBC's Malcolm Nance took to Twitter to denounce Glenn Greenwald as a treasonous "agent of Trump and Moscow" for traveling to a conference in Russia and speaking with several Russian people. Nance, who usually just makes things up, was actually telling the truth this time. Greenwald really did visit Russia, and was selfied in the company of Edward Snowden, on top of which he's totally gay, and God knows what kind of Commie orgies go on in the Kremlin dungeon!

And the neoliberal Resistance was just getting started. As Trump was arriving at Stansted Airport to begin his "destruction of British diplomacy"[6] (and possibly poison the Queen with more of that Novichok oatmeal that has been plaguing the UK), *The Guardian*'s Owen Jones was personally preparing cells of the London Resistance for "the biggest demonstration in British history,"[7] or "the biggest weekday protest in British history,"[8] or a very large protest in any event.

The London Resistance's secret weapon was the Baby-Russian -Agent-Hitler Blimp,[9] which forced Trump and his Nazi goons to retreat to one of his Scottish golf resorts, but not before humiliating America, and horrifying *The Washington Post*, by failing to grovel before the British monarch.[10] Still, the point is, London was saved. The forces of hatred, bigotry, and Russianness were roundly defeated by

5 Chait, Jonathan, "Will Trump Be Meeting With His Counterpart — Or His Handler?" New York Magazine, July 9, 2018

6 Smith, David, "Trump leaves London after wreaking diplomatic destruction," The Guardian, July 13, 2018

7 Eleftheriou-Smith, Loulla-May, "Anti-Trump protest group hoping for 'biggest demonstration in British history' if US President makes UK trip," The Independent, December 4, 2017

8 Owen Jones on Twitter, "Is the biggest weekday protest in British history?" July 13, 2018

9 Mackintosh, Eliza and Fox, Kara, "'Trump Baby' balloon takes flight in London protests," CNN, July 13, 2018

10 Hassan, Jennifer, "Did Donald Trump just WALK IN FRONT OF THE QUEEN?" Washington Post, July 13, 2018 (caps in the original WaPo headline)

the forces of love, and goodness, and democracy, and tolerance, and whatever. If only the French had been willing to deploy a baby Hitler blimp in 1940 … or had been able to unite the corporate media, the Intelligence agencies, the capitalist ruling classes, and thousands of virtue-signaling liberals to disapprove of the original Hitler!

But that wasn't all … oh no, far from it. No, the weeks of white-eyed editorials warning us of the dangers of peace, the neo-McCarthyite smear campaigns, the virtue-signaling Stop-Trump protests, all that was just an extended edition of Orwell's famous Two Minutes Hate, designed to generate mass hysteria and paranoia in the run-up to the summit.

By Friday, the US Intelligence Community was issuing warnings of imminent Russian "attempts to undermine America" with September 11 scale "cyber attacks!" National Intelligence Director Dan Coats personally told the *Associated Press* that the little "Imminent Russia Attack" lights he has on his desk were all "blinking red."[11] Apparently, Trump and the Putin-Nazis are preparing "a crippling cyber attack" against "critical US infrastructure," like "a power outage in New England in January," or even "a cyber attack on banks" that will erase Americans' entire life savings but somehow spare all the Russian accounts, or at least another devastating round of division-sowing Facebook ads!

Then, just in time for the corporate media to milk it throughout the weekend, special counsel Robert Mueller, III released a 29-page indictment accusing a bunch of Russian spies of … well, basically, being Russian spies. The indictment alleges that these Russian spies destroyed the campaign of Hillary Clinton, who everyone knows is supposed to be President, by "hacking" the Democratic Party's servers and stealing and disseminating emails revealing both Clinton and the Democratic Party to be the soulless neoliberal hypocrites most people already knew they were.

The indictment of these Russian intelligence officers (and no Americans nor any other parties who can ever actually be brought to trial, requiring special counsel Mueller to offer evidence to support his allegations) was followed up by a chorus of voices demanding

11 Riechmann, Deb, "Intel official: Cyber threat warnings 'blinking red'," Associated Press, July 13, 2018

that the summit be cancelled and that Trump slink home in complete disgrace to confess his crimes to a vindicated nation, and then presumably fire his entire administration, resign, and appoint Hillary Clinton President.[12]

Sometime early Sunday morning, after hours of careful deliberation over cheeseburgers and sodas on Air Force One with the Gorilla Channel streaming on his smartphone for ambiance, Trump decided to go ahead with the summit. This left the Resistance no other choice than to turn up the dial on the manufactured hysteria by repeating the words "treason," "treasonous," and "traitor" as many times as humanly possible on every news site, television channel, and social media platform in existence, and just generally running around like lunatics shrieking about an "IMMINENT RUSSIAN ATTACK!"

On the morning of the summit, Charles M. Blow, maestro of alliteration and subtlety, in *The New York Times* (which, we must remember, holds itself to the highest journalistic standards and in no way resembles a rabble-rousing tabloid), published this impassioned piece entitled "*Trump, Treasonous Traitor*," accusing the President of "betraying the nation," and basically demanding that he be tried for treason.[13] "America is under attack," Blow announced, "and its president absolutely refuses to defend it."

And, if *Mother Jones*' David Corn has his way, Senator Rand Paul, who Corn denounces as "a traitor,"[14] would also be taken outside and shot for the crime of noting that the Attack on America® Russia allegedly perpetrated is fairly standard clandestine behavior, engaged in by most developed nations, including the United States of America, whose history of election interference, coup-fomenting, assassinations, and other, more hamfisted forms of regime change is common knowledge, or at least it was, until the ruling classes and the corporate media turned the majority of Western liberals into paranoid McCarthyite fanatics denouncing anyone who questions

---

12 Shabad, Rebecca, "Dems call on Trump to cancel Putin summit after Russian hacking indictments," NBC News, July 13, 2018

13 Blow, Charles M., "Trump, Treasonous Traitor," The New York Times, July 15, 2018

14 See Glenn Greenwald's tweet of July 16, 2018, featuring a screenshot of Corn's "TRAITOR" tweet, which of course Corn promptly deleted.

the honesty of the US Intelligence Community as a "traitor," and seeing Russians and Nazis coming out of the woodwork.

In the wake of Trump's Treasonous Traitor Summit, which Garry Kasparov has called "the darkest hour in the history of the American presidency"[15] (i.e., darker than Truman dropping the bomb on Hiroshima and Nagasaki), the neoliberal establishment and the corporate media appear to have gone full Joe McCarthy. Virtually every establishment mouthpiece, former spook, official state clown, from Thomas Friedman to Stephen Colbert, have been braying about "treason" and "traitorousness," and suggesting that Donald Trump be removed from office by … you know, whatever means necessary.

At least David Frum, senior editor at *The Atlantic*, had the balls to openly call for a CIA-orchestrated military coup, because we can't afford to wait for the legal process to take its course this time, as we are "facing a national security emergency!"[16]

God knows where we go from here. It's hard to believe the ruling classes can keep teasing liberals, and other Trump-obsessives, over and over and over like this, without eventually impeaching or shooting the guy. But, then again, maybe they can. Perhaps they intend to continue conducting this experiment all the way up to 2020, just to see how paranoid and mindlessly conformist they make the majority of the Western public.

In any event, if they decide not to impeach him, and then try him for treason, or just kill him, or whatever, the Democrats at least have a new campaign slogan that they can use in 2018 and beyond …

> "NEXT TIME VOTE FOR WHO WE TELL YOU TO,
> YOU RUSSIA-LOVING NAZI SCUM!"

Kind of has a ring to it, doesn't it?

---

15 Garry Kasparov on Twitter, July 16, 2018 ("I'm ready to call this the darkest hour in the history of the American presidency. Let me know if you can think of any competition.")

16 Frum, David, "The Crisis Facing America," The Atlantic, July 16, 2018

Where Have All the Nazis Gone?

August 17, 2018

So it appears Antifa has scared Trump's army of emboldened Nazis back into their hidey holes, or at least that's the spin the Resistance is putting on the deeply weird events of last Sunday. In case you missed it, what happened was, thousands of "anti-fascist" protestors converged on the streets of the nation's capitol to deny a platform to (or just beat the snot out of) twenty or thirty racist idiots who were trying to assemble in Lafayette Square and stand around shouting racist slogans at each other.

The organizer of this idiotic fiasco (i.e., the racist fiasco, not the protest thereof) was the same attention-seeking, racist idiot that had organized the original "Unite the Right" event in Charlottesville in 2017. During that weekend, as I'm sure you'll recall, a white supremacist drove his car into a crowd of protesters, killing a woman, numerous other people were assaulted, and a few hundred racists in polo shirts and khakis marched around with tiki torches hollering neo-Nazi gibberish in an attempt to launch some sort of race war, or protest the removal of a statue, or something.

Last Sunday was a little less dramatic. Basically, these twenty or thirty racists were escorted by hundreds of riot police and Secret Service to Lafayette Square, where they found themselves surrounded by thousands of protesters, many of whom intended to stomp their guts out. This must have been a bit unsettling, because the racists reportedly fled their own "rally" before they'd even had the chance to holler any Nazi gibberish at each other.

This was extremely disappointing for the militant "anti-fascist" contingent, which had been counting on another balls-out street fight. According to *The New York Times*,[1] a group of frustrated mil-

---

1 Fausset, Richard, "Rally by White Nationalists Was Over Almost Before It Began," The New York Times, August 13, 2018

itant types tried to burn a Confederate flag, but it wouldn't catch fire, despite several attempts, so they were forced to rip it apart with their hands and throw it on the ground and jump up and down on it. Other militant "anti-fascists" threw anti-Nazi eggs at the cops, presumably as a form of "preventative self-defense," or just to ensure that *Breitbart* had some video to paint them as "terrorists" with. The not-quite-so-militant "anti-fascist" contingent, most of whom never even caught a glimpse of the "emboldened" Nazis they had come to resist, apparently dispersed without incident.

The corporate media and the rest of the Resistance had been flogging this event for months. That infamous photo of the tiki torch Nazis[2] had been repeatedly reprinted all summer long. Features on Kessler, the organizer (whose activities seem to have been mostly funded by his grandmother, with whom he had also been living) had been published in major international broadsheets. The coverage peaked going into the weekend. On Saturday, he was featured on National Public Radio, where he shared his views on "racial intelligence." (Go ahead, google him, and marvel at the amount of free publicity bestowed on this geek.)

And it wasn't just the corporate media. No, the militant "anti-fascist" left had also been also promoting this so-called "rally" as the Return of the Revenge of the Bride of Charlottesville. Affinity groups had been activated. "Anti-fascist" posters had been printed. Militant Twitter hashtags created. Snappy "anti-fascist" slogans, like "It takes a bullet to bash the fash," and "Drive out Trump/Pence fascist regime," had been applied to colorful signs and banners. By Sunday morning, social media was buzzing with thousands of tweets and posts by people hoping to "punch a Nazi." Antifa was obviously looking forward to some hardcore "preventative self-defense" ... all they needed were a few hundred Nazis.

So, it was a little embarrassing, to put it mildly, when only a dozen or two racists showed up, instead of the hordes of swastika-tattooed, Sieg-heiling Nazis the Resistance was hoping for. After all the energy and money they've invested in convincing millions of credulous liberals that America is being existentially threatened by

2 Wilson, Jason, "Charlottesville: far-right crowd with torches encircles counter-protest group," The Guardian, August 12, 2017

legions of fascists "emboldened" by Trump (and somehow connected to Vladimir Putin), to then have this paltry bunch of racist misfits show up for "the big Nazi rally" ... well, it kind of makes a mockery of the official narrative they've been selling everyone.

According to that official narrative, which the global capitalist ruling classes and the corporate media have been disseminating since Hillary Clinton lost the election, America and democracy are under attack by a vast conspiracy of Russians and Nazis (I've been referring to them as "the Putin-Nazis"), nominally led by Donald Trump, but actually controlled by Vladimir Putin, who is desperately trying to annihilate "the West" and establish a Russian-Nazi Empire which he will personally rule with an iron fist.

As the story goes, back in 2015, Putin and his Russian Nazis, infuriated at us for fomenting a coup with our Ukrainian Nazis on their southern border, finally activated Donald Trump, who they had recruited back in the 1980s (and then blackmailed with a sex tape twenty years later), and who had been posing as a narcissistic billionaire ass clown while awaiting the "go code" from his handlers in Moscow.

Trump sprang immediately into action, announcing his candidacy on June 16, and set about "emboldening" the millions of American Nazis who had been patiently waiting for the day when a racist New York real estate huckster would rise from the depths of reality television to lead them to victory in RaHoWa ... or whatever. Up until Trump announced his run, these American Nazis had been keeping a low profile by having swastikas tattooed on their faces, flying Confederate flags in their yards, burning crosses, posting calls for genocide on Nazi websites, and occasionally murdering people of color and bombing churches and daycare centers. Once Trump hit the hustings, however, the Nazis abandoned all restraint and got right down to the business of posting Nazi frogs on social media, touring campuses with Nazi book tours, and gathering in upscale Italian restaurants to be photographed mimicking Hitler-salutes.

All this emboldenment culminated in the infamous rally in Charlottesville last summer, which, as the Resistance pointed out, was just like Kristallnacht ... except that Charlottesville was not a pogram and ninety-one Jewish people weren't murdered. But, aside from that, it was exactly the same. Trump emboldened it, then openly condoned it, and given that he's a Russian agent, we can assume the orders came directly from Putin, who presumably has agents in the fascist underground, possibly in Kessler's grandmother's basement, and who's been randomly poisoning people in Salisbury (i.e., Putin has, not Kessler's grandmother), and possibly orchestrating Jeremy Corbyn's Nazification of the Labour Party, and who has been influencing people with Facebook posts, and God knows what other horrors he's been up to … at this point, it's hard to keep it all straight.

In any event, after the Charlottesville Kristallnacht, the Resistance went to work hunting down Nazis, getting them arrested or fired from their jobs, or just showing up at their pathetic little gatherings and stomping the living Hitler out of them. Being mostly idiots, they weren't hard to find, at least not the tiki torch Kessler variety. We're not talking the Aryan Brotherhood here. We're talking about creeps like the "Crying Nazi,"[3] Richard Spencer[4] (another media darling), Andrew Auernheimer[5] (a/k/a "weev"), groups like the Proud Boys (who you've probably never heard of unless you travel in "anti-fascist" circles), and other such idiots who have absolutely nothing to do with actual power in the United States, or anywhere else.

Which, of course, is the point of the Nazi hysteria the Resistance has been barraging us with, that is, when they are not too busy barraging us with the Trump-is-a-Russian-Agent hysteria. As I've outlined in several other essays, there is no "Russian Attack on Democracy," nor is there any "blood-dimmed tide" of emboldened Nazism menacing the West. All that is really happening is, the global capitalist ruling classes are conducting a counterinsurgency PSYOP, the objective of which is to put down "populist" resistance to the spread of global capitalism. There is no clutch of global capitalists sitting in a room conspiring to do this. It is simply the system responding (as a system) to eliminate an internal threat, and reestablish control of its environment, which in this case happens to be the whole planet.

---

3 Spencer, Hawes, "'Crying Nazi' Christopher Cantwell Says He's Just a 'Goddamn Human Being'," The Daily Beast, August 30, 2017

4 "Richard Spencer: Five Things to Know," Anti-Defamation League, March 29, 2018

5 Gutman, Rachel, "Who Is Weev, and Why Did He Derail a Journalist's Career?" The Atlantic, February 14, 2018

One part of this counterinsurgency PSYOP is delegitimizing anyone and anything that stands in the way of global capitalism. It does not matter one iota whether the opposition stems from what most of us think of as the "Left" or the "Right." Global capitalism does not care. It simply cannot have major disruptions like the Brexit referendum and the election of Trump screwing with its Privatization of Everything (which it began in the early 1990s, immediately after the end of the Cold War). Such populist insurgencies feed each other. One day, it's the nationalists abandoning the EU, the next day, it's socialists boycotting Israel, the day after that it could be Americans demanding universal healthcare, subsidized college education, or demilitarization of the nation's police. Things could get out of control pretty quickly.

The other part of this counterinsurgency PSYOP is manufacturing as much mass hysteria and paranoia about Russian agents and emboldened Nazis as humanly possible. This aspect of the PSYOP sells itself... opposing global capitalism is difficult work and not very rewarding. It's so much easier (and much more fun) to hunt down imaginary Russians and Nazis. And if you don't know any Russian operatives, or can't find any actual Nazis, no worries, there are plenty of Assad-apologists, Putin-apologists, Alex Jones-apologists, terrorist-apologists, transphobic racists, anti-Semitic British socialists, and crypto-Red-Brown fascist entryists, not to mention Susan Sarandon and everyone else who didn't vote for Clinton. You can hunt them down and call them names on Facebook from the comfort of your home. I'm relatively sure the Internet monitors at the Atlantic Council[6] won't mind if you do. Just watch what you say about the CIA, the FBI, the NSA, and the other valiant corporations and non-governmental organizations that are "working together to secure the future."

Oh, and if you do see any of those actual Nazis crawling up out of their hidey holes, or anyone who looks they might be about to commit an act of verbal genocide, go ahead and gouge their eyes out or something ... because we can't afford to give these Nazis an inch.

Have a nice day, and happy hunting!

---

6 Breland, Ali, "Facebook partners with Atlantic Council to improve election security, The Hill, May 17, 2018

Putin-Nazi Paranoia

September 13, 2018

They're out there … Trump-loving, Assad-apologist, Putin-Nazi sleeper agents, posing as regular normal Americans. They could be anyone. They could be your neighbors, the guys in the copy room, your Uber drivers, even some of your Twitter followers. They're sitting there, right now, glued to their televisions, waiting for Jewish Nazi law clerks to perform a series of secret hand signs, blinks, hiccups, sneezes, coughs, and almost undetectable, low-frequency flatulence that will signal the launch of the "Attack on America."

It could come at any moment now.

Zina Bash is definitely one of them. Don't let her Mexican-Jewish ancestry, or the fact that her grandparents were Holocaust survivors, fool you into thinking otherwise. She made that "OK" sign at the Kavanaugh hearings,[1] which, all right, apparently wasn't the cue for the millions of American Putin-Nazis to rip off their rubbery masks of normality and storm into the streets in their polo shirts singing "Tomorrow Belongs to Me" … but it was some kind of secret Nazi code!

Certainly, Alex Jones is one of them. Why else would patriotic global corporations like Apple, Facebook, Twitter, and YouTube suddenly ban him from all their platforms after allowing him to spew his bile there for years?[2] It's probably only a matter of time until Google's "algorithms" unperson him entirely, at which point I'll receive instructions to delete any reference to him in this essay, or risk being further deranked myself.

I will, of course, comply immediately, as no one despises Alex Jones more than I, even though, oddly, I've never watched him. Thank God for that, as who knows how my mind could have been permanently

---

1 Tacopino, Joe, "Conspiracy about woman at Kavanaugh hearing rages online," New York Post, September 4, 2018 ("A former clerk to Supreme Court nominee Brett Kavanaugh was accused by Twitter trolls of using a 'white supremacist' symbol — even though the woman is of Mexican and Jewish heritage.")

2 Chappell, Bill and Tsioulcas, Anastasia, "YouTube, Apple and Facebook Ban Infowars, Which Decries 'Mega Purge'," National Public Radio, August 6, 2018

warped by whatever Nazi content he's been forcing less fortunate Americans to consume!

And then, God help us, there's Jeremy Corbyn and his genocidal communist Nazi Death Cult![3] If he isn't one of them, no one is. If you haven't been following the British media, the story is, basically, that Jeremy Corbyn is a terrorist-loving, anti-Semitic, conspiracy theorizing, racist traitor to everything the British ruling classes stand for, and has transformed the U.K. Labour Party into a homicidal mob of Jew-hating brownshirts. Gangs of slavering Corbyn-Nazis are roving the lanes of Kensington and Knightsbridge accusing Jews of "lacking irony" and saying mean things about the State of Israel.

British Jews have been advised to flee the country[4] or to shelter in place until the tabloids, *The Guardian*, the ruling classes, and Tony Blair can hound this Hitlerian devil out of office ... which, the way things are going, should be any day now.

Meanwhile, the British soldier on under the imminent threat of Putin-Nazi Novichok perfume assassin hit squads, which Putin could send at any moment directly from Moscow to Gatwick Airport to incompetently attempt to murder their targets by spraying the deadliest nerve agent in existence onto the doorknobs of their suburban homes and then stroll around getting filmed by every CCTV camera in Britain.[5] As far as I know, the British tabloids haven't yet published surveillance photos of Corbyn welcoming the Skripal assassins at Gatwick with a wreath, or a bottle of Stolichnaya (and wearing his Russian-stooge hat,[6] of course), but I won't be terribly shocked when they do.

And the Putin-Nazis are not just on the march in the United States and Great Britain. They're coming out of the woodwork in Europe! As I'm sure you're aware, here in Germany, in a city called Chemnitz in the Free State of Saxony, which has never had any kind of Nazi problems (except for the fact that the entire region has been

3 Hopkins, C. J., "Jeremy Corbyn's Nazi Death Cult," Consent Factory, April 6, 2018

4 Embury-Dennis, Tom, "Labour antisemitism causing British Jews to consider leaving country, says leading rabbi," The Independent, August 2, 2018

5 Harding, Luke, "Planes, trains and fake names: the trail left by Skripal suspects," The Guardian, September 5, 2018

6 Oppenheim, Maya, "Newsnight denies photoshopping Jeremy Corbyn image to make Labour leader look Russian," The Independent, March 18, 2018

infested with neo-Nazis for decades and is generally known here as Neo-Nazi Central), thousands of just regular foreigner-hating Volk joined a few hundred neo-Nazis in marching around with German flags, barking xenophobic slogans, heiling Hitler, harassing assorted "non-German-looking" human beings, and various other forms of "protest."

Such unprecedented eruptions of Nazism occur on a regular basis in Saxony, albeit on a smaller scale, so it was rather awkward for the corporate media to link the events in Chemnitz to Trump, but nevertheless they managed to sneak a few references to his "emboldenment" in. The best they could do to tie in to Putin was to publish a lot of photos of skinheads hanging around that humongous statue of Marx in the center of Chemnitz's central square, because, you know, Putin, Trump, Marx, Stalin, Assad, Saddam, Gaddafi ... whoever, they're all just different brands of Hitler!

Seriously, though, all comedy aside ... I have to hand it to David Brock, or Jennifer Palmieri, or whoever it was that came up with the Putin-Nazi narrative. OK, granted, the Putin part hasn't quite worked, except on die-hard Obama disciples, Hillary-worshippers, and other bull-goose loonies, but the Nazi stuff is going gangbusters ... and not just with the liberal public (because that has always been an easy sell), but also with the more leftist left.

It has taken a while, but we have arrived at the point where even "hardcore anti-capitalist leftists" are dedicating most of their time and energy to calling Donald Trump a fascist, and likening him to Hitler, and so on, over and over, and over again, in increasingly exasperated tones. Why, in Marx's name, these leftists want to know, won't other leftists join the chorus of voices screaming, "TRUMP IS A FASCIST!" in all caps on a daily basis? How could these other leftists not see that this is not the time to attack the corporate media, the Intelligence community, global corporations, or anyone other than DONALD TRUMP, who is LITERALLY ADOLF FUCKING HITLER?

Anthony DiMaggio's recent essay in *CounterPunch*[7] is a prime example of the effect the Putin-Nazi paranoia is having on leftists.

7 DiMaggio, Anthony, "Full-On Fascism: Trump Makes the Transition in his War on the Press," CounterPunch, September 11, 2018

According to DiMaggio, Donald Trump, by tweeting mean things about Attorney General Sessions and bombastically threatening *The New York Times*, is no longer just a normal fascist. He is now officially a "full-on fascist," or a "real-world fascist," or a super duper fascist!

DiMaggio doesn't have any qualms about the deep state, or rather, the "steady state,"[8] sabotaging an elected president (or at least pretending to be doing do so in print), because … well, you know, "the stakes are far higher" than mere democracy, what with Hitler in the White House. (William Kristol would agree wholeheartedly.[9])

But calling Trump a fascist again is just an overture for DiMaggio's main theme, which is that it's time to unite the left against the growing Putin-Nazi threat. See, the problem is not just the Putin-Nazis. It is also the fellow Putin-Nazi travellers, and the Assadists, and the Red-Brown infiltrators! Yes, you know who we are, do you not? Glenn Greenwald is our leader, naturally, but Caitlin Johnstone is second-in-command. We refer to her in our secret meetings as "Caity, Queen of the Putin-Nazis."

DiMaggio links to a helpful list of other traitorous Strasserist spies compiled by the crackpot Louis Proyect, folks like Norman Finkelstein, Mike Whitney, Diana Johnstone, Patrick Cockburn, Tom Engelhardt, and Michael Hudson, whose essays have been published in *The Unz Review*, which also publishes a lot of "alt-right," racist, and anti-Semitic essays. (Full disclosure: Proyect contacted me, demanding to know how I can allow my work to appear on a Nazi website like Unz, but I ignored him, as I assumed he was just trolling me, again, but it appears he was fishing for incriminating comments for his groundbreaking piece of investigative journalism.

8 Moss, Bradley P., "The 'Steady State' Is Shirking Its Obligations," The Atlantic, September 6, 2018 ("The recent publication in The New York Times of an anonymous op-ed by a 'senior official in the Trump administration" brings into sharp relief the extent to which various members of the Trump administration are not just knowingly working to curb the president's recklessness, but are doing so based in part upon the belief that those impulses are the result of something deeper and more fundamentally unstable about the man himself. I long had assumed the president was prone to childish tantrums and had little time and less inclination to understand the mechanics of governance. I was nonetheless skeptical of the legitimacy of concerns about his mental or psychological health, especially when assessed from afar. Such concerns should never be haphazardly invoked. The op-ed, though, claims that a cadre of senior appointees—which it dubs the 'steady state'—has taken it upon itself to steer the government through choppy waters of erratic presidential behavior.")

9 William Kristol on Twitter, "Obviously strongly prefer normal democratic and constitutional politics. But if it comes to it, prefer the deep state to the Trump state," February 14, 2017

In any event, I seem to have escaped inclusion on his Red-Brown blacklist. For the record, I'm with Norman Finkelstein. I don't stop anyone from reposting my essays, no matter what I think of their other contributors. I wouldn't even stop *The New York Times* from publishing my stuff, though, of course, they never would … and *they* publish actual mass-murdering war criminals.)

Anyway, according to Anthony DiMaggio:

> "Leftists who focus on the propagandistic nature of the corporate media while shilling for the far right and failing to condemn right-wing fascism provide comfort to the reactionary right's efforts to suppress journalistic freedom."

Well, Jesus, I wouldn't want to do anything like that. I hope DiMaggio will follow up with a breakdown of exactly how many times I need to call Donald Trump a fascist before I am allowed to criticize the propagandistic nature of the corporate media, or the global capitalist ruling classes, or any type of "full-on fascism" that doesn't neatly fit into his simplistic category … like the type that seeks to impose a regime of anus-puckering ideological conformity on those it determines are members of its camp, and that gets off punishing deviations from its norms.

Look, the truth is, I don't like Donald Trump. I haven't liked him for about thirty years. I have no problem whatsoever with leftists like DiMaggio calling him names until they're blue in the face if that makes them happy.

What I do find troubling is the growing atmosphere of neo-McCarthyite paranoia which has been gradually spreading into leftist quarters, and the witch-hunting, and the Putin-Nazi-baiting, and the compiling and distributing of pseudo-blacklists, and the cheering on of global corporations as they ideologically sterilize the Internet.

We get enough of that from the corporate media. So how about we lighten up on the paranoia, let the global capitalist ruling classes finish destroying Donald Trump, and maybe think about what the Left has to offer as an alternative to the global-corporate, post-"fascist," neo-feudal future.

While it might not feel like it at the moment, it's coming … we'll be there before you know it.

N.B. This was my final essay for *CounterPunch*, which had been reposting my columns for over two years. Following its publication, *CounterPunch*'s editors, Jeffrey St. Clair and Joshua Frank (possibly at the behest of Louis Proyect, who, although not officially an editor, appears to wield considerable power at *CounterPunch*), dropped my columns, ignored my inquiries, and then attempted to smear me as an "anti-Semite." Their basis for smearing me as an "anti-Semite" was that I wouldn't forbid Ron Unz (*a man from whom the CounterPunch editors have taken approximately $100,000 over the years*) to repost my columns in *The Unz Review*. I documented this strange and ugly episode in a subsequent essay, "*How to Maliciously Smear Your Critics (and Not Get Away with It)*," which is not included in this volume, but is available on the Consent Factory blog and in assorted other online publications.

Down with the Working Classes!

September 21, 2018

If the Left is ever going to come together to save the world from Donald Trump and his legions of fascistic Putin-Nazis, we're going to need to confront our primary enemy … the international working classes. Yes, comrades, I'm afraid it's time to face the facts, depressing as they are. The working classes are not our friends. Just look at how they've been betraying us … and after all we've done for them all these years! This cannot be allowed to continue, not if we are going to rescue democracy from Trump, Putin, Assad, the Iranians, and Palestinian kids with terrorist kites, and eventually stem the blood-dimmed tide of neo-fascist anti-Globalism!

Now, OK, I know you're probably asking, "how can the international working classes possibly be the enemy of the Left?" and "wouldn't that render the whole concept of the Left completely absurd and essentially meaningless?" and other pertinent questions like that. And that's totally fine, you're allowed to ask that. Questioning aspects of the official narrative the ruling classes are forcing everyone to conform to like members of a worldwide cult doesn't make you a Nazi or anything. It's perfectly OK to ask such questions, as long as you don't continue to ask them, over and over, and over again, after the facts have been explained to you.

Here are those facts, one more time.

The international working classes are racists. They are misogynists. Xenophobic transphobes. They do not think the way we want them to. Some of them actually still believe in God. They are white supremacists. Anti-Semites. Gun-toting, Confederate-flag-flying rednecks. Most of them have never even heard of terms like "intersectionality," "TERF," and so on. They do not respect the corporate media. They think that news sources like *The Washington Post*, *The New York Times*, *The Guardian*, CNN, MSNBC, BBC, and so on, are basically propaganda outlets for the global corporations and oligarchs who own them, and thus are essentially no different from FOX, whose pundits they believe every word of. Their minds are so twisted by racism and xenophobia that they can't understand how global capitalism, the graduated phase-out of national sovereignty, the privatization of virtually everything, the debt-enslavement of nearly everyone, and the replacement of their so-called "cultures" with a ubiquitous, smiley-faced, gender-neutral, non-oppressive, corporate-friendly Disney simulation of culture are actually wonderfully progressive steps on the road to a more peaceful, less offensive world.

Now this has been proved in numerous studies with all kinds of charts and graphs and so on. And not only by the corporate statisticians, and the corporate media, and liberal think tanks. Why, just this week, Mehdi Hasan, in an exasperated jeremiad in the pages of *The Intercept*,[1] that bastion of fearless, adversarial journalism owned by billionaire Pierre Omidyar, proved, once again, that Donald Trump was elected because PEOPLE ARE GODDAMN RACISTS!

Apparently, Hasan has just about had it with these Putin-loving Trump-apologists proposing that general dissatisfaction with global capitalism, neoliberalism, and identity politics could have had anything to do with Americans electing a bombastic ass clown with absolutely no political experience to the highest office in the land.

Hasan cites a number of expert studies, among them one by the "Democracy Fund," which just happens to be another Omidyar outfit. But let's not get all paranoid or anything. There are literally hundreds of such studies at this point, each and every one of which has been cited by the mainstream media, the alternative media, the far-alternative media, and virtually every Trump-obsessed loon with a blog or a Facebook or Twitter account.

Look, I realize the truth is painful, but the science of statistics leaves no room for doubt. As much as some of us may want to deny it, the fact is, the country that elected Barack Obama (who is Black) president, twice, has been transformed by Putin's brainwashing agents into a cesspool of xenophobia and racism, and it is up to us lefties to set things right!

1 Hasan, Mehdi, "Time to Kill the Zombie Argument: Another Study Shows Trump Won Because of Racial Anxieties — Not Economic Distress," The Intercept, September 18, 2018

Now, to do this, we need to unite the Left, and get everyone marching in lockstep, and so on. Which means that we need to identify and weed out all the fake leftists among us. Then, and only then (i.e., after we've tracked down, sanctimoniously denounced, and exiled any and all neo-Stasserist "alt-Right" infiltrators, Sputnik leftists, and Assad-apologists), can we turn our attention to meeting face-to-face with the international working classes and sanctimoniously denouncing them as a bunch of filthy racists.

OK, that sounds a little harsh, and possibly totally idiotic, but what other choice do we lefties have? If we're going to defeat these Putin-Nazis, a few eggs are going to have to get broken. This is not the time to abandon our commitment to imposing our identity-based ideology on every last person on the planet Earth, or to indulge in that ugly kind of old-fashioned leftism that is based on what the working classes want. Who gives a damn what the working classes want? What's important is what we want them to want. This isn't the 1990s, after all. All that nonsense about globalization, and supranational entities like the WTO, and the World Bank, not to mention "American jobs" ... only fascists talk like that these days!

But, seriously, if you've made it this far in my essay, and you consider yourself a leftist of some sort, you're probably extremely frustrated with what passes for the Left these days, and with how the working classes are flocking to the Right, both in the United States and all over the world. If I've got that right, you might want to read this essay by Diana Johnstone[2] (which we lefties are technically not allowed to read, because it's posted in *The Unz Review*, where a lot of "alt-Right" pieces are also posted ... and you don't want to get any of that stuff on you!).

What she is writing about is the ongoing "populist" backlash, or insurgency, against global capitalism, which is what I've also been writing about for the better part of the last two years. This is the historical moment we are experiencing, a clumsy, sloppy, partly fascistic, partly non-fascistic democratic uprising against the continuing spread of global capitalism, the erosion of what is left of national sovereignty, and ... yes, people's cultures and values.

2 Johnstone, Diana, "Disobedient Hungary: from the Soviet to the European Union," The Unz Review, September 17, 2018

The working classes understand this. The neo-nationalist Right understands this. The majority of the Left does not understand this, and is refusing to admit that it's happening, and is standing around on the sidelines calling everybody "racists" and "fascists" while the global capitalist ruling classes and the neo-nationalists sort things out.

Which is exactly what the ruling classes want, and what the official "Putin-Nazi" narrative was designed to achieve from the very beginning. The "Overton Window" (i.e., the range of ideas tolerated in public discourse) works best when divided into two clean halves. During the so-called "War on Terror," it was Democracy versus the Islamic Terrorists. Now, it's Democracy versus the Putin-Nazis. Both of which narratives are fairy tales, of course, the reality, as ever, being rather more messy.

If what is left of the Left expects to play any meaningful part in this historical moment (other than sanctimoniously cheerleading for the global capitalist ruling classes), it is going need to get its hands a little dirtier, and mingle a bit more with all those working class "populists," and talk to them, and ... I don't know, maybe even listen to them.

Or perhaps I'm completely out of my mind. I mean, *listening* to the working classes? Some of them are sure to say racist things, and anti-Semitic and transphobic things, which we cannot ignore, not even for one second, or rationally discuss and disagree with, because that would mean giving their racism a platform, and ...

Never mind, screw it, I don't know what I was thinking. Forget all that stuff I just made you read.

Down with the fascist working classes!

Who Doesn't Love Identity Politics?

October 8, 2018

If there is one thing that still unites Americans across the ever more intellectually suffocating and bitterly polarized political spectrum our imaginations have been crammed into like rush hour commuters on the Tokyo Metro, it's our undying love of identity politics.

Who doesn't love identity politics? Liberals love identity politics. Conservatives love identity politics. Political parties love identity politics. Corporations love identity politics. Advertisers, anarchists, white supremacists, Wall Street bankers, Hollywood producers, Twitter celebrities, the media, academia …

Everybody loves identity politics.

Why do we love identity politics? Well, we love them for many different reasons.

The ruling classes love identity politics because they keep the working classes focused on race, ethnicity, gender, sexual orientation, religion, and so on, and not on the fact that they (i.e., the working classes) are, essentially, glorified indentured servants, who will spend the majority of their sentient existences laboring to benefit a ruling elite that would gladly butcher their entire families and sell their livers to hepatitic Saudi princes if they could get away with it.

Dividing the working classes up into sub-groups according to race, ethnicity, and so on, and then pitting these sub-groups against each other, is extremely important to the ruling classes, who are, let's remember, a tiny minority of intelligent but physically vulnerable parasites controlling the lives of the vast majority of human beings on the planet Earth, primarily by keeping them ignorant and confused.

The political parties love identity politics because they allow them to conceal the fact that they are bought and paid for by these ruling classes, which, in our day and age, means corporations and a handful of obscenely wealthy oligarchs who would gut you and your kids like trout and sell your organs to the highest bidder if they thought they could possibly get away with it.

The political parties employ identity politics to maintain the simulation of democracy that prevents Americans (many of whom are armed) from coming together, forming a mob, dismantling this simulation of democracy, and then attempting to establish an actual democracy, of, by, and for the people, which is, basically, the ruling classes' worst nightmare.

The best way to avoid this scenario is to keep the working classes ignorant and confused, and at each other's throats over things like pronouns, white privilege, gender appropriate bathrooms, and the complexion and genitalia of the virtually interchangeable puppets the ruling classes allow them to vote for.

The corporate media, academia, Hollywood, and other elements of the culture industry are similarly invested in keeping the vast majority of people ignorant and confused. The folks who populate this culture industry, in addition to predicating their sense of self-worth on their superiority to the unwashed masses, enjoy spending time with the ruling classes, and reaping the many benefits of serving them, and, while most of them wouldn't personally disembowel your kids and sell their organs to some dope-addled Saudi trillionaire scion, they would look the other way while the ruling classes did, and then invent some sort of convoluted rationalization of why it was necessary, in order to preserve democracy and freedom (or was some sort of innocent but unfortunate "blunder," which will never, ever, happen again).

The fake Left loves identity politics because they allow them to pretend to be "revolutionary" and spout all manner of "militant" gibberish while posing absolutely zero threat to the ruling classes they claim to be fighting. Publishing fake Left "samizdats" (your donations to which are tax-deductible), sanctimoniously denouncing racism on Twitter, milking whatever identity politics scandal is making headlines that day, and otherwise sounding like a slightly edgier version of National Public Radio, are all popular elements of the fake-left repertoire.

Marching along permitted parade routes, assembling in designated "free speech areas," and listening to speeches by fake-left celebrities and assorted Democratic Party luminaries, are also well-loved fake -left activities. For those who feel the need to be even more militant, pressuring universities to cancel events where potentially "violent" and "oppressive" speech acts (or physical gestures) might occur, toppling offensive historical monuments, ratting out people to social media censors, or masking up and beating the crap out of "street Nazis" are among the available options.

All these activities, by herding potential troublemakers into fake Left ghettos and wasting their time, both on- and off-line, help to ensure that the ruling classes, their political puppets, the corporate media, Hollywood, and the rest of the culture industry can keep most people ignorant and confused.

Oh, and racists, and hardcore white supremacists, and anti-Semites, and other far-Right wing nuts ... my God, do they love identity politics! Identity politics are their entire worldview (or Weltanschauung, for you Nazi fetishists). Virtually every social, political, economic, and ontological phenomenon can be explained by reducing it to race, ethnicity, religion, or some other simplistic criterion, according to these "alt-right" geniuses. And to render everything even more simplistic, each and every one of their simplistic theories can be subsumed into a meta-simplistic theory, which amounts to (did you guess it?) a conspiracy of Jews.

According to this meta-theory, this conspiracy of Jews (which is headquartered in Israel, but maintains offices in Los Angeles and New York, from which it controls the corporate media, Hollywood, and the entire financial sector) is responsible for ... well, anything they can think of. September 11 attacks? Conspiracy of Jews. Financial crisis? Jews, naturally. Black on Black crime? Jews again! Immigration? Globalization? Gun control laws? Abortion? Drugs? Media bias? Who else could be behind it all but Jews?!

See, the thing is, there is no essential difference between your identity politics-brainwashed liberal and your swastika-tattooed white supremacist. Both are looking at the world through the lens of race, gender, sexual orientation, religion, or some other type of "identity." They are looking through this "identity" lens (whichever one it happens to be) because either they have been conditioned to do so (most likely from the time they were children) or they have made a conscious choice to do so (after recognizing, and affirming or rejecting, whatever conditioning they received as children).

Quantum physicists, Sufi fakirs, and certain other esoterics understand what most of us don't, namely, that there is no such thing as "the Truth," or "Reality," apart from our perception of it. The world, or reality, or whatever you want to call it, is more than happy to transform itself into any imaginable shape and form, based on the lens you are looking at it through. It's like a trickster in that regard. Look at "reality" through a racist lens, and everything will make sense according to that logic. Look at it through a social justice lens, or a Judeo-Christian lens, or a Muslim lens, or a scientific or a Scientologist lens, or a historical materialist or capitalist lens (it really makes no difference at all) ... and abracadabra! A new world is born!

Sadly, most of us never reach the stage in our personal (spiritual?) development where we are able to make a conscious choice about which lens we want to view the world through. Mostly, we stick with the lens we were originally issued by our families and societies. Then we spend the rest of our fleeting lives desperately insisting that our perspective is "the Truth," and that other perspectives are either "lies" or "errors." The fact that we do this is unsurprising, as the ruling classes of whatever society we happened to be born and socialized into are intensely invested in issuing everyone a "Weltanschauung lens" that corresponds to whatever narrative they are telling themselves about why they deserve to be the ruling classes, and why we deserve to exist to serve them, fight their wars, pay interest on their loans, not to mention rent to live on the Earth, which they have claimed as their own and divided up amongst themselves to exploit and ruin, which they justify with "laws" they invented, which they enforce with armies, police, and prisons, which they teach us as children to believe is "just the way life is" ... but I digress.

So, who doesn't love identity politics? Well, I don't love identity politics. But then I tend to view political events in the context of enormous, complex systems operating beyond the level of the individuals and other entities such enormous, complex systems comprise. Thus I've kind of been keeping an eye on the restructuring of the planet by global capitalism that started in the early 1990s, following the collapse of the USSR, when global capitalism (not the USA) became the first globally hegemonic system in the history of aspiring hegemonic systems.

Now, this system (i.e., capitalism, not the USA), being globally hegemonic, has no external enemies, so what it's been doing since it became hegemonic is aggressively destabilizing and restructuring the planet according to its systemic needs (most notably in the Middle East, but also throughout the rest of the world), both militarily and ideologically. Along the way, it has encountered some resistance, first, from the Islamic "terrorists," more recently, from the so-called "nationalists" and "populists," none of whom seem terribly thrilled about being destabilized, restructured, privatized, and debt-enslaved by global capitalism, not to mention relinquishing what remains of their national sovereignty, and their cultures, and so on.

I've been writing about this for over two years, so I am not going to rehash it all in detail here (this essay is already rather long). The short version is, what we are currently experiencing (i.e., Brexit, Trump, Italy, Hungary, et cetera, the whole "populist" or "nationalist" phenomenon) is resistance (an insurgency, if you will) to hegemonic global capitalism, which is, essentially, a values-decoding machine, which eliminates "traditional" (i.e., despotic) values (e.g., religious, cultural, familial, societal, aesthetic, and other such non-market values) and replaces them with a single value ... exchange value, thus rendering everything a commodity.

The fact that I happen to be personally opposed to some of those "traditional" values (e.g., racism, anti-Semitism, oppression of women, homosexuals, and so on) does not change my perception of the historical moment, or the sociopolitical, sociocultural, and economic forces shaping that moment. God help me, but I believe it might be more useful to attempt to understand those forces than to go around pointing and shrieking at anyone who doesn't conform to my personal views like the pod people in *Invasion of the Body Snatchers*.

But that's the lens I choose to look through. Maybe I've got it all assbackwards. Maybe what is really going on is that Russia "influenced" everyone into voting for Brexit and Donald Trump, and hypnotized them all with those Facebook ads into hating women, people of color, transsexuals, and the Jews, of course, and all that other "populist" stuff, because the Russians hate us for our freedom, and are hell-bent on destroying democracy and establishing some kind of neo-fascist, misogynist, pseudo-Atwoodian dystopia.

Or, I don't know, maybe the other side is right, and it really is all a conspiracy of Jews ... transsexual, immigrant Jews of color, who want to force us all to have late-term abortions and circumcise our kids, or something.

I wish I could help you sort all that out, but I'm just a lowly political satirist, and not an expert on identity politics or anything. I'm afraid you'll have to pick a lens through which to interpret reality yourself. But then, you already have, haven't you ... or are you still looking through the one that was issued to you?

The Putin-Nazi-Terrorist-O-Matic

October 29, 2018

I suppose it was always just a matter of time until the global capitalist ruling classes and their mouthpieces in the corporate media combined their two main official narratives into a Ronco-type 2-in-1 kind of deal. That's right, folks, your days of switching between the War on Terror official narrative and the Putin-Nazi official narrative are over, because now, for just $19.99, the Putin-Nazi-Terrorist-O-Matic® takes care of all your official narrative needs with just the press of one button!

Here's how it works. First, you take your classic mentally-disturbed individual, someone like, say, John Hinkley, Jr., Mark David Chapman, Travis Bickle, or a total wack job like Cesar Sayoc, and you paint whichever clearly psychotic crimes he's committed as acts of "terrorism." Don't worry about the definition of "terrorism" or how it has become a virtually meaningless label the capitalist ruling classes and corporate media can slap onto anyone. Just keep saying "terrorist," "terrorism," and any other lexical derivatives of "terror," over and over, like some kind of mantra ... you know, like the Hare Krishnas do.

Next, you take whatever obsession your disturbed individual is maniacally obsessed with, and you paint that obsession as an "ideology," or some kind of organized political movement, as if your wack job was actually a rational person and not just a totally paranoid geek who decided to attempt to assassinate Reagan because he couldn't get a date with Jodie Foster, or to murder John Lennon because God had instructed him to do so in a J. D. Salinger novel.

Now, this works much better if your disturbed individual is actually obsessed with something political, like, say, if he's a Donald Trump fanatic who has plastered the windows of the van he's living in with all sorts of blatantly psychotic artwork deifying Donald Trump and demonizing Donald Trump's political opponents, but you'll have to work with what your lunatic gives you.

In any event, whatever his pathology, you will need to de-pathologize your psycho, so that you can misrepresent him as a "domestic terrorist," and then associate whatever "ideology" you've just painted onto him with "terrorism."

If that sounds a little complicated, don't worry, folks, it's really not! The ruling classes and the corporate media just provided us with a demonstration of the Putin-Nazi-Terrorist-O-Matic in action, which proves how easy-to-use it is.

In the span of just a single week, they whipped up so much mass paranoia that, by the weekend, millions of hysterical liberals were calling for a deep-state coup, and the arrest and internment of all registered Republicans, because a right-wing loon had sent a bunch of non-exploding bomblike devices to prominent members of the neoliberal "Resistance," or rather, to their respective mail-screening services.[1]

These Putin-Nazi-Terrorist "bomb-like devices" were "intercepted" throughout last week. Their targets were a roll call of Resistance heroes, Soros, Obama, Hillary Clinton, John Brennan, the offices of CNN, Eric Holder, Maxine Waters, Joe Biden, and, yes, even Robert De Niro! Putin-Nazi panic paralyzed the nation! The neoliberal corporate media (who, remember, are serious, respected professionals, not conspiracist nuts like Alex Jones) began pouring out pieces informing the world that Donald Trump was behind these attacks, or had encouraged, "emboldened," or "inspired" whoever was with his violent, neo-Hitlerian rhetoric.

The Washington Post went full Shakespearean with Dana Milbank's "What Hath Trump Wrought?"[2] *The New York Times* explained how Trump was employing a strategy called "stochastic terrorism," i.e.,

1 Dienst, Jonathan, Winter, Tom, Williams, Pete, and Silva, Daniella, "Some mailed pipe bombs could have been duds, investigators say," NBC News, October 25, 2018 (At least some of the devices found in the wave of suspected pipe bombs mailed to prominent political and media figures had no possibility of exploding -- because they contained flaws in the way they were made, several investigators told NBC News on Thursday, based on early analysis. In a few cases, the flaws were substantial, the investigators said.)

2 Milbank, Dana, "What hath Trump wrought?" Washington Post, October 24, 2018

inspiring random acts of violence that are statistically predictable but individually unpredictable![3] "Trump's words have consequences," *The Guardian* lectured.[4] "Words matter," CNN concurred.[5] John Brennan, who courageously continued to appear on television despite the ongoing threat, affirmed that Trump's "un-American" rhetoric had "emboldened individuals to take matters into their own hands."[6] Even "alternative" Resistance outlets like *Truthout* joined the chorus of voices reporting that "Trump's Rhetoric Emboldens Violence!"[7]

By Thursday morning, #MAGAbomber, #MAGATerrorist, and other such hashtags were circulating widely on Twitter. Which meant that it was only a matter of time until the Resistance linked these stochastically-terrorist-MAGA-bomber attacks to Russia.

On Thursday evening, MSNBC's Chuck Todd did exactly that, speculating that "this could be a Russian operation!"[8] *Washington Post* propagandist Craig Timberg, author of the infamous McCarthyite smear piece on "peddlers of Russian propaganda"[9] that got the whole "fake news" hysteria started back in December 2016, would soon follow up with a ridiculous attempt to connect the "MAGA Terrorist" to Russia by exposing the alleged "pro-Kremlin views" he allegedly "echoed" in some Facebook posts[10] … but I'm getting a little ahead of myself.

By Friday, after anti-Terrorism specialists (or the kids that work in the mail-screening room) "intercepted" more "bomb-like devices" addressed to Senator Cory Booker and ex-National Intelligence

---

3 Press, Eyal, "This Week's Mail Bombs Are No Surprise," The New York Times, October 25, 2018

4 Younge, Gary, "Trump's words have consequences, and he can no longer deny it," The Guardian, October 25, 2018

5 Avlon, John, "Here's how many times Trump attacked pipe bomb targets," CNN, October 26, 2018

6 Kelly, Caroline, "John Brennan calls Trump's rhetoric 'un-American' in first remarks after bomb scare," CNN, October 25, 2018

7 Goodman, Amy, "Pipe Bombs Point to How Trump's Rhetoric Emboldens Violence," Truthout, October 25, 2018

8 Correll, Diana Stancey, "Chuck Todd floats theory suspicious packages may be part of 'Russian operation'," Washington Examiner, October 25, 2018

9 Timberg, Craig, "Russian propaganda effort helped spread fake news during election, experts say," The Washington Post, November 24, 2016

10 Timberg, Craig and Romm, Tony, "Mail bomb suspect made numerous references on Facebook to Russian associates and echoed pro-Kremlin views," Washington Post, October 27, 2018

Director James Clapper, the neoliberal punditocracy were soiling themselves on national television. This was it! The long-awaited Putin-Nazi Apocalypse had finally begun, and just as Paul Krugman had prophesied it would![11] ... or, OK, not exactly like that, but still, Trump was, once again, about to suspend the Constitution, declare martial law, and appoint himself dictator! Clearly, Putin had ordered Trump to launch the destruction of Western democracy by deploying the dreaded Totally-Incompetent-Domestic-Terrorist-Mail-Bomber Strategy ... and just in time for the midterm elections!

And then, just like that, they caught him. Cesar "the Jackal" Sayoc, Jr., the terrorist mastermind that had nearly perpetrated another 9-11-type event, and who was sleeping in his van behind an auto parts store! As is standard procedure for terrorist sleeper agents, Sayoc, until he was "activated," had been maintaining a totally low-profile cover as juiced-up, body-building, racist male stripper with an extensive criminal record and an obsession with Trump. Like the "Skripal assassins" and other Putin-Nazi operatives, he had made a point of getting himself photographed and noticed by witnesses in various public places, and otherwise drawing attention to himself, which is one of the first things they teach you at the Kremlin. Sayoc hasn't yet divulged the names and ranks of his handlers in the GRU, but, presumably, Eliot Higgins and Bellingcat are hard at work googling that right this minute.

In the meantime, the liberal corporate media have been working the Putin-Nazi-Terrorist-O-Matic on a more or less 24/7 basis. It is crucial at a time like this, when mass hysteria is reaching peak levels, that the public not be allowed to believe that this "MAGA Terrorist" is merely one more pathetic, attention-seeking geek who decided to vent his impotent rage on those he perceived as his mortal enemies.

---

11 Paul Krugman, prophesying in a 4-part Twitter thread: "(1) If Democrats don't at least take the House, God help us. But even if they do, we'll be facing a nightmarish political scene. Republicans will claim that the election was stolen, and deny the majority's legitimacy. (2) Democrats will gain subpoena power - but expect the Trump administration to simply defy requests for information, the way they already are on issues like the Mar-a-Lago crowd's influence on the Veterans Administration. (3) They'll also probably abuse executive power in many other ways. And they'll use claims of voter fraud to justify their disregard of the law and Constitution. If you don't think this is going to happen, you haven't been paying attention. (4) In the very near future, many government officials will probably face hard decisions about whether to defy illegal orders from their political superiors. And remember, this is the good scenario."

Same goes for the Pittsburgh synagogue attacker, who struck as I was writing this piece. Never mind that this homicidal idiot did not like Trump, who he condemned as a "Jew-lover."[12] In order to maintain the official narrative, the ruling classes need us to believe that he was not just another anti-Semite with a gun collection and a gab.com account, but, rather, an official "domestic terrorist," who was probably "radicalized" by Donald Trump's rhetoric![13]

Look, I'm no fan of Donald Trump, or racism, or anti-Semitism (despite what my smear-happy former editors at *CounterPunch* would like you to believe).[14] What I am is a student of the production of ideology. I lived through the deployment of the official "War on Terror" narrative after 9-11, and then watched in frustration as millions of Americans mindlessly supported a war of aggression, the abrogation of many of their civil liberties, torture, and various other atrocities, based on nothing but propaganda and media-generated mass hysteria.

We're experiencing a similarly historic ideological readjustment at the moment, which I've been trying to capture (satirically and more seriously) since it began in the summer of 2016. The official "War on Terror" narrative (and people's understanding of what "terrorism" is) is being gradually redefined and expanded to encompass any and all forms of "extremism" (i.e., whatever the ruling classes decide is "extremism"). Mass murder, battery, racist graffiti, opposing the spread of global capitalism, saying nasty things about Soros, tattooing your forehead with a giant swastika, using the words "globalism," "sovereignty," and so on … the distinctions are rapidly disappearing.

The media-generated mass hysteria over Islamic terrorism during the War on Terror is being replaced with media-generated mass hysteria over Nazis and Russians (unless you're a die-hard Trump supporter, in which case, you've got your immigration hysteria, but my focus is on ruling class ideology, which, despite the existence of Donald Trump, remains neoliberal, supranational, and, yes, God

12 Connelly, Eileen AJ, "Alleged gunman's anti-Semitic views revealed in social media posts," New York Post, October 27, 2018

13 Byman, Daniel, "When to Call a Terrorist a Terrorist," Foreign Policy, October 27, 2018

14 Hopkins, C. J., "How to Maliciously Smear Your Critics (and Not Get Away with It)," Consent Factory, October 5, 2018

help me, globalist in nature). Any and all forms of opposition to global capitalist ideology, regardless of whether they come from the Left or the Right, are being stigmatized as "extremism," and thus inextricably linked to "terrorism." I described this, back in January, as a global capitalist "War on Dissent,"[15] and I think events over the last ten months have largely confirmed my diagnosis.

I'd love to go on, but this essay is already way too long for people's phones, and the midterm elections are fast approaching, so this is no time for critical thinking … and plus, news is just coming in from *Guardian* contributor Christina Patterson that Jeremy Corbyn and the Labour Party are also responsible for the Pittsburgh attack,[16] and for "emboldening" all these "extremists" and "terrorists," and for "normalizing" anti-Semitism and fascism, and mass murder, and who knows what other atrocities, and I don't want to miss a chance to catch the Putin-Nazi-Terrorist-O-Matic in action!

---

15 Hopkins, C. J., "The War on Dissent," Consent Factory, January 26, 2018

16 Wright, James, "It didn't take a Guardian contributor long to smear Jeremy Corbyn with the Pittsburgh massacre, live on Sky News," The Canary, October 28, 2018

Oceania is at War with Fascism

November 5, 2018

If you're a critic of global capitalism (also referred to as "globalism"), I've got some good news and some bad news for you. The good news is, you're not a "peddler of Russian propaganda" anymore.[1] The bad news is, you're an anti-Semite.

You're probably also a domestic terrorist, or an "emboldener" of domestic terrorism, or at least some sort of terrorism-apologist. And not good old-fashioned Islamic terrorism like we used to get during the War on Terror, because that ended in the Summer of 2016, right around the time Trump won the nomination. No, the brand of terrorism you are probably emboldening by criticizing global capitalism is anti-Semitic, fascist terrorism ... the most terroristic form of terrorism there is!

Up until recently, you might have just been going about your normal business, criticizing global capitalism, completely unaware of your anti-Semitic, white supremacist terrorist activities, but from now on there will be no denying them. Your hate thoughts are right there for everyone to read. Go back and check your Facebook posts and your Twitter feed. You'll see what I mean. All those times when you impulsively lashed out against the global capitalist ruling classes, or globalism, or Obama, or Clinton, or the Wall Street banks, or, God help you, George Soros[2] ... well, you might as well have been tweeting blinking neon GIFs of dancing swastikas or posting Adolf Hitler's speeches with little throbbing hearts and smiley-face emoticons.

According to the "Anti-Fascist Resistance" (i.e, the the Democratic

---

1 *Timberg, Craig, "Russian propaganda effort helped spread fake news during election, experts say," The Washington Post, November 24, 2016*

2 *Lavin, Talia, "Conspiracy theories about George Soros aren't just false. They're anti-Semitic," Washington Post, October 24, 2018*

Party, the Intelligence community, the corporate media, those Wall Street banks, the military-industrial complex, and other components of the global capitalist empire that doesn't actually exist, except as a Nazi "conspiracy theory"), any references you might have made to "globalists," or "globalism," or the "corporate media," or "banks," or "Hollywood," or the "1 percent," or any other "elites," didn't really refer to what they referred to, but, in fact, were anti-Semitic "dog whistles." If you went so far as to literally mention or include an unflattering photo of Soros in any of your posts or tweets, then you weren't just "whistling" to your fascist dog friends, you were openly calling for a second Holocaust, or "inspiring" some anti-Semitic psycho to senselessly murder a bunch of people, as recently happened at that synagogue in Pittsburgh.[3]

This newly rebranded "Anti-Fascist Resistance" (formerly known as the "Anti-Putin Resistance," that is, until pre-election polling convinced them that most Americans were not responding to their "Russiagate" propaganda)[4] has been working more or less around the clock to badger the public into believing that this psycho was an official "lone wolf terrorist," and that "America is on the brink of fascism,"[5] and that Trump is "deploying the fascist playbook,"[6] and that attacking the media is "the first step toward fascism,"[7] and that Trump is a fascist because he isn't a fascist (or something ... I couldn't quite make sense of that one),[8] and, basically, that everyone should be afraid of fascism![9]

---

3 "Pittsburgh shooting: What we know so far," BBC, October 28, 2018 ("A gunman entered the Tree of Life synagogue in Pittsburgh on Saturday morning and opened fire, killing 11 people.")

4 Maté, Aaron, "With Just Days to the Midterms, Russiagate Is MIA," The Nation, October 28, 2018

5 Frantz, Douglas, "Is Trump driving the U.S. toward the brink of fascism?" The Globe & Mail, November 1, 2018

6 Tharoor, Ishan, "Trump deploys the fascist playbook for the midterms," Washington Post, November 1, 2018

7 Staff, "Jane Fonda: Trump shares parallels with 'rise of Third Reich and Adolf Hitler'," The Guardian, November 2, 2018

8 Snyder, Timothy, "Donald Trump borrows from the old tricks of fascism," The Guardian, October 30, 2018 ("If Trump is not a fascist, this is only in the precise sense that he is not even a fascist. He strikes a fascist pose, and then issues generic palliative remarks and denies responsibility for his words and actions. But since total irresponsibility is a central part of the fascist tradition, it is perhaps best to give Trump his due credit as an innovator.")

9 "If you're not scared about fascism in the U.S., you should be," The New York Times, October 15, 2018 (A video by Jason Stanley)

Like that scene in Orwell's *1984* when the Party abruptly switches official enemies in the middle of the Hate Week rally, the Resistance is counting on its loyal members to instantly forget the Russia hysteria they have been mindlessly parroting for almost two years and start mindlessly parroting Fascism hysteria (as they mindlessly parroted the Terrorism hysteria throughout the Global War on Terror, until they switched to parroting the Russia hysteria after Trump got elected in 2016).

This recent rebranding of the neoliberal Resistance was a brilliant move, and is going quite well. It couldn't have come at a better time, what with the midterm elections about to take place. While liberals were ready to swallow any anti-Trump narrative the corporate media rammed down their throats from the moment Clinton lost, much of the slightly-more-left-leaning Left never bought the Russiagate story. So it's been tough for slimy Beltway operatives like David Brock and other propagandists to unite "the Left" behind the Democratic Party, so they can put down this annoying "populist" insurgency, reinstall some Obama-like puppet, and get back to the business of globalism ... no, not worldwide Jewish domination, you Jew-obsessed, neo-Nazi freaks, but, rather, the consolidation of corporate control over what remains of society, the abrogation of national sovereignty, and the establishment of a smiley, happy, multicultural, over-medicated, neo-feudal global capitalist marketplace.

This Fascism hysteria is doing the trick!

This is the beauty of the "Putin-Nazi" narrative, which was designed to be a one-two punch. First, they hit us with the "Russiagate" hysteria, which worked like a charm on the kind of liberals who have no qualms about destroying whole countries, murdering hundreds of thousands of people in faraway lands that pose zero threat to us, and debt-enslaving millions of Americans to enrich the global investor classes, as long as someone like Obama is doing it. Then, once all the NPR liberals had been whipped into a hysterical frenzy over "Russian propaganda," "collusion," and so on, they hit us with the Fascism hysteria, which is working like a charm on the rest of the Left. (I haven't seen any official polling, but when the official narrative is being mindlessly parroted, not only by the liberal corporate media, but also by "grassroots" left-wing outlets like *Truthout*,

Democracy Now, and *CounterPunch*, you know their propaganda is working.)

Not that there aren't a bunch of racists, anti-Semites, and other bigots out there. Of course there are. There always have been, just as there have always been terrorists out there (or non-state militants, depending on your perspective). Some of these racists and anti-Semites are obviously homicidal lunatics. This is not a new phenomenon. The American white supremacist fringe (and, sorry, but it is still a fringe) has been shooting and bombing innocent people, and otherwise doing their utmost to get their ridiculous "Racial Holy War" going since at least the early 1970s, and arguably since end of the Civil War. They have been doing this without any "emboldenment" from billionaire jackasses like Donald Trump, and they will continue to do this once Trump is gone and this Fascism hysteria has outlived its usefulness ... like the War on Terror hysteria did.

If you're in the mood to live a bit dangerously and want a preview of what that will be like, switch off your smartphone for a minute, turn off the television, shut down the notebook, and walk out into the city, suburb, town, or gated community you live in. Does it look like the Nazis have taken over?

OK, want to live even a little more dangerously? And I'm talking about flirting with serious thoughtcrime. Ask yourself, how many actual terrorists did you encounter during the War on Terror (that is, assuming you didn't invade their country and start, you know, bombing and shooting at them)? Can you even remember as far back as July, when Oceania was at war with Russia, and Trump (temporarily) wasn't Hitler, but was a treasonous "Russian intelligence asset," who was almost certainly going to disband NATO, and a "crippling Russian cyber attack" on vital American infrastructure was imminent?

I doubt it, because that never happened.

Oceania has never been at war with Russia. Oceania is at war with Fascism. Oceania has always been at war with Fascism. Donald Trump has always been Hitler. He has never been a Russian intelligence asset. Obama never put children in cages,[10] or assassinated

10 Perper, Rosie, "Side-by-side photos show migrant children locked up in cages under both Trump and Obama," Business Insider, July 21, 2018

entire families at weddings.[11] Trump's nativism leads to anti-Semitism.[12] America is not a safe place for Jews.[13] The invasion of Iraq was just a tragic mistake, which will never, ever, happen again. There are no global capitalist elites, and anybody who says there are is an anti-Semite and a fascist thoughtcriminal, and an emboldener of domestic terrorism, which is "a plague America can no longer ignore."[14] Oh, yeah, and I almost forgot, the Ministry of Plenty has just announced that there will be no reduction of the chocolate ration. The chocolate ration will be increased!

So don't forget to vote blue tomorrow and help the Party defeat the fascists! Or, if you're one of the fascists, don't forget to vote red tomorrow and help the Party save America from that Jewish Mexican zombie horde that is coming to steal your fruit-picking job!

And whatever you do, stay tuned to the telescreen, and do not start thinking about global capitalism, or the manufacture of mass hysteria, or put anything into any kind of broader historical or geopolitical context. That kind of thinking leads straight to thoughtcrime ... and we all know where thoughtcrime leads.

---

11 Ackerman, Spencer, "41 men targeted but 1,147 people killed: US drone strikes – the facts on the ground," The Guardian, November 24, 2014 ("Finally, on 15 October 2010, Hellfire missiles fired from a Predator or Reaper drone killed Hussain, the Pakistani Taliban later confirmed. For the death of a man whom practically no American can name, the US killed 128 people, 13 of them children, none of whom it meant to harm.")

12 Beinart, Peter, "How Trumpian Nativism Leads to Anti-Semitism," The Atlantic, November 2, 2018

13 Milbank, Dana, "Trump's America is not a safe place for Jews," Washington Post, October 28, 2018

14 Bergen, Peter, "Homegrown terrorism: A plague we cannot ignore," CNN, October 28, 2018

The Indiscreet Charm of the Gilets Jaunes

December 11, 2018

So it appears the privatization of France isn't going quite as smoothly as planned. As I assume you are aware, for over a month now, the gilets jaunes (or "yellow vests"), a multiplicitous, leaderless, extremely pissed off confederation of working-class persons, have been conducting a series of lively protests in cities and towns throughout the country to express their displeasure with Emmanuel Macron and his efforts to transform their society into an American-style neo-feudal dystopia. Highways have been blocked, toll booths commandeered, luxury automobiles set on fire, and shopping on the Champs-Élysées disrupted. What began as a suburban tax revolt has morphed into a proper working-class uprising.

It took a while for "the Golden Boy of Europe" to fully appreciate what was happening. In the tradition of his predecessor, Louis XVI, Macron first responded to the gilets jaunes by inviting a delegation of *Le Monde* reporters to laud his renovation of the Élysée Palace, making the occasional condescending comment, and otherwise completely ignoring them.[1]

That was back in late November. Last Saturday, he locked down central Paris, mobilized a literal army of riot cops, "preventatively arrested" hundreds of citizens, including suspected "extremist students,"[2] and sent in the armored military vehicles.[3]

The English-language corporate media, after doing their best

---

1 Pietralunga, Cédric, "A l'Elysée, coup de jeune sur les ors de la République," Le Monde, November 30, 2018

2 "France protests: Footage of students 'humiliated' by police," BBC, December 7, 2018 ("Footage of school students being forced to kneel with their hands behind their heads by French riot police has sparked outrage on social media. Police said that those arrested at the Saint-Exupery school were suspected of taking part in an 'armed gathering', adding that officers had wanted to break up a situation that was getting 'out of control', Le Monde newspaper reported.")

3 O'Connor, Tom, "France Sends In Military Vehicles Used in War Zones to Take On Paris 'Yellow Vests' Protests," Newsweek, December 7, 2018

not to cover these protests (and, instead, to keep the American and British publics focused on imaginary Russians), have been forced to now begin the delicate process of delegitimizing the gilets jaunes without infuriating the the entire population of France and inciting the British and American proletariats to go out and start setting cars on fire. They got off to a bit of an awkward start.

For example, this piece by Angelique Chrisafis,[4] *The Guardian*'s Paris Bureau Chief, and her Twitter feed from the protests last Saturday. Somehow (probably a cock-up at headquarters), *The Guardian* honchos allowed Chrisafis to do some actual propaganda-free reporting, and some interviews with actual protesters,[5] before they caught themselves and replaced her with Kim Willsher, who resumed *The Guardian*'s usual neoliberal establishment-friendly narrative,[6] which, in this case, entailed dividing the protesters into "real" gilets jaunes and "fake" gilet jaunes, and referring to the latter fictional group as "thuggish, extremist political agitators."

By Sunday, the corporate media were insinuating that diabolical Russian Facebook bots had brainwashed the French into running amok, because who else could possibly be responsible? Certainly not the French people themselves! The French, as every American knows, are by nature a cowardly, cheese-eating people, who have never overthrown their rightful rulers, or publicly beheaded the aristocracy. No, the French were just sitting there, smoking like chimneys, and otherwise enjoying their debt-enslavement and the privatization of their social democracy, until they unsuspectingly logged onto Facebook and ... BLAMMO, the Russian hackers got them!

---

4 Chrisafis, Angelique, "'Macron's arrogance unites us' – on the barricades with France's gilets jaunes," The Guardian, December 7, 2018

5 A Twitter thread by Chrisafis, December 7, 2018 ("Some in Paris have suggested all gilets jaunes are driven by fake-news and conspiracy theories on Facebook, & are somehow uneducated. That was not what I found and it would be a mistake to think that. I met people who had in the past run their own small companies (building/maintenance), some who worked in the public sector (school assistants, nurses), or who were self-employed or skilled. They knew the tax system inside out, they had been paying in as bosses and workers, there was a sophisticated level of political debate and an exasperation. A few had voted Macron and were disappointed. There was big range of political views on the same barricade – from leftwingers and ecologists opposed to nationalism, to people who had voted for nationalism in the form of Marine Le Pen. All said they were united in fury at Macron's way of running France – what they called his top-down approach cut off from ordinary people's experiences. Everyone could angrily quote examples of Macron's 'arrogance'...")

6 Willsher, Kim, "Police flood into Paris to contain gilets jaunes," The Guardian, December 7, 2018

Bloomberg is reporting that the French authorities have opened a probe into Russian interference[7] (in the middle of which report, for no apparent reason, a gigantic photo of Le Pen is featured, presumably just to give it that "Nazi" flavor). According to "analysis seen by *The Times*," Russia-linked social media accounts have been "amplifying" the "chaos" and "violence"[8] by tweeting photos of gilets jaunes who the French police have savagely beaten or gratuitiously shot with "less-than-lethal projectiles." "Are nationalists infiltrating the yellow vests?" the BBC Newsnight producers are wondering.[9] And, according to *Buzzfeed*'s Ryan Broderick, "a beast born almost entirely from Facebook"[10] is slouching toward ... well, I'm not quite sure, the UK or even, God help us, America!

And then there's Max Boot, who is convinced he is being personally persecuted by Russian agents like Katie Hopkins, James Woods, Glenn Greenwald, and other high-ranking members of a worldwide conspiracy Boot refers to as the "Illiberal International" (but which regular readers of my column will recognize as the "Putin-Nazis").[11]

And this is the problem the corporate media and other defenders of global neoliberalism are facing with these gilets jaunes protests. They can't get away with simply claiming that what is happening is not a working-class uprising, so they've been forced to resort to these blatant absurdities. They know they need to delegitimize the gilets jaunes as soon as possible, as the movement is already starting to spread, but the "Putin-Nazi" narrative they've been using on Trump, Corbyn, and other "populists" is just not working.

---

7 Matlack, Carol and Williams, Robert, "France to Probe Possible Russian Influence on Yellow Vest Riots," Bloomberg News, December 8, 2018

8 Blakely, Rhys, "Russian accounts fuel French outrage online," The Times, December 8, 2018

9 "Gilets Jaunes: Are nationalists infiltrating the 'yellow vests'?" - BBC Newsnight, December 7, 2018

10 Broderick, Ryan and Darmanin, Jules, "The 'Yellow Vest' Riots In France Are What Happens When Facebook Gets Involved With Local News," Buzzfeed, December 5, 2018

11 Boot, Max, "In France and online, extremists put centrism to the torch," Washington Post, December 10, 2018 ("On Dec. 3, amid pictures of burning cars and tear gas in Paris, I woke up to find incessant Twitter criticism of an article I'd written. This was hardly shocking; I'm attacked online all the time ... I was struck by how many versions of the same criticism were repeated by anonymous trolls, and it made me wonder if Russian bots were involved. When I suggested as much in a tweet, I earned a rebuke from the right-wing British conspiracy-monger Katie Hopkins, who has lost her Mail Online column but retains 882,000 Twitter followers: 'The world thinks you are a cockwomble, sir. If you are looking for someone to blame — find a mirror darling.'")

No one believes the Russians are behind this, not even the hacks who are paid to pretend they do. And the "fascism" hysteria is also bombing. Attempts to portray the gilets jaunes as Le Pen-sponsored fascists blew up in their faces. Obviously, the far-right are part of these protests, as they would be in any broad working-class uprising, but there are far too many socialists and anarchists (and just regular pissed-off working-class people) involved for the media to paint them all as "Nazis."

Which is not to say that the corporate media and prominent public intellectuals like Bernard-Henri Lévy[12] will not continue to hammer away at the "fascism" hysteria, and demand that the "good" and "real" gilets jaunes suspend their protests against Macron until they have completely purged their movement of "fascists," and "extremists," and other dangerous elements, and have splintered it into a number of smaller, antagonistic ideological factions that can be more easily neutralized by the French authorities ... because that's what establishment intellectuals do.

We can expect to hear this line of reasoning, not just from establishment spokespersons like Lévy, but also from the Identity Politics Left, who are determined to prevent the working classes from rising up against global neoliberalism until they have cleansed their ranks of every last vestige of racism, sexism, homophobia, xenophobia, transphobia, and so on.

These leftist gatekeepers have been struggling a bit to come up with a response to the gilets jaunes ... a response that doesn't make them sound like hypocrites. See, as leftists, they kind of need to express their support for a bona fide working-class uprising. At the same time, they need to delegitimize it, because their primary adversaries are fascism, racism, sexism, homophobia, xenophobia, and assorted other isms and phobias, *not* the neoliberal ruling classes.

Nothing scares the Identity Politics Left quite like an actual working-class uprising. Witnessing the furious unwashed masses operating out there on their own, with no decent human restraint whatsoever, identity-politics leftists feel a sudden overwhelming urge to analyze, categorize, organize, sanitize, and otherwise correct

12 Lévy, Bernard-Henri, "Will the Yellow Vests Reject the Brown Shirts?" Project Syndicate, December 5, 2018

and control them. They can't accept the fact that the actual, living, breathing working classes are messy, multiplicitous, inconsistent, and irreducible to any one ideology. Some of them are racists. Some are fascists. Others are communists, socialists, and anarchists. Many have no idea what they are, and don't particularly care for any of these labels.

This is what the actual working classes are ... a big, contradictory collection of people who, in spite of all their differences, share one thing in common, that they are being screwed over by the ruling classes. I don't know about you, but I consider myself one of them.

Where we go from here is anyone's guess. According to *The Guardian*, as I am sitting here writing this, the whole of Europe is "holding its breath" in anticipation of the gilets jaunes' response to Macron's most recent attempt to appease them, this time with an extra hundred Euros a month, some minor tax concessions, and a Christmas bonus.[13]

Something tells me it's not going to work, but even if it does, and the uprising ends, this messy, Western "populist" insurgency against global neoliberalism has clearly entered a new phase. Count on the global capitalist ruling classes to intensify their ongoing war on dissent, and their demonization of anyone opposing them, or contradicting their official narrative, as an "extremist," a "fascist," a "Russian agent," and so on.

I'm certainly looking forward to that, personally.

Oh, yeah, and I almost forgot, if you were wondering what you could get me for Christmas, I did some checking, and there appears to be a wide selection of yellow safety vests online for just a couple Euros.

13 Henley, Jon, "Europe holds its breath as Macron scrambles to quell protests," The Guardian, December 10, 2018

The Year of Putin-Nazi Paranoia

December 19, 2018

As my regular readers will probably recall, according to my personal, pseudo-Chinese zodiac, 2017, *anno Domini*, was "The Year of the Headless Liberal Chicken."[1]

This year, having given it considerable thought, and having consulted the I Ching, and assorted other oracles, I'm designating 2018 "The Year of Putin-Nazi Paranoia."

Not that 2017 wasn't already paranoid. It was. It was completely paranoid, and otherwise clinically batshit crazy. But 2018 has been batshit crazier.

It started out with the Internet companies that control the flow of information that most of us now perceive as reality launching an all-out War on Dissent, purportedly to protect the public from "divisive" and "confusing" content, and other forms of Russian "influencing."

Twitter started sending out scary emails warning customers that there was "reason to believe" that they had "followed," "retweeted," or "liked the content of" accounts "connected to a propaganda effort by a Russian-government-linked organization."[2] Facebook launched its own Ministry of Truth, manned by "a dedicated counter-terrorism team" of "former intelligence and law-enforcement officials" (a/k/a The Atlantic Council, NATO's unofficial propaganda wing).[3] And Google stepped up its covert deranking of insufficiently Russia-hating and other "non-authoritative" websites.[4]

---

1 Hopkins, C. J., "The Year of the Headless Liberal Chicken," Consent Factory, December 8, 2017

2 O'Sullivan, Donie, "Twitter to tell 677,775 people they interacted with Kremlin-linked trolls," CNN Business, January 19, 2018

3 Hedges, Chris, "Thought Police for the 21st Century," Truthdig, January 21, 2018 ("Monika Bickert, head of global policy management at Facebook, told the U.S. Senate Committee on Commerce, Science, and Transportation in a hearing Wednesday that Facebook employs a security team of 10,000 -- 7,500 of whom 'assess potentially violating content' -- and that 'by the end of 2018 we will more than double' it to over 20,000.")

4 "Google to 'derank' Russia Today and Sputnik," BBC, November 21, 2017

This Orwellian corporate censorship campaign was enthusiastically welcomed by liberals and other Russia-and-Trump-obsessives, who by this time were already completely convinced that secret Russian Facebook agents were conspiring to transform the Western masses into zombified, Russia-loving neo-Nazis by means of some sort of irresistible Putin-Nazi hypno-technology that would melt their brains to oatmeal the second they clicked on one of those dancing cat GIFs.

But the paranoia was just getting started. By the Spring, professional Putin-Naziologists were issuing warnings explaining that anyone using words like "globalist," or "globalism," or "global capitalism" was an anti-Semite. There was no such thing as "globalism," they told us. "Globalist" was just Nazi codespeak for "JEW!" Moreover, anyone criticizing "the media," or mentioning "banks," "Wall Street," or "Hollywood," or, God help you, making fun of "George Soros," was clearly a Russia-loving, Sieg-heiling Nazi.

Meanwhile, in London, Blairites were busy combing through six year-old Facebook posts in an effort to prove that Jeremy Corbyn had transformed the British Labour Party into his personal Putin-Nazi death cult. *The Guardian* published over one hundred articles smearing Corbyn as an anti-Semite and "linking" Labour to anti-Semitism.[5] The BBC jacked up the Russia paranoia, doctoring Corbyn's hat on TV to make it appear more insidiously Slavic.[6] Owen Jones sprang to Corbyn's defense,[7] explaining that, yes, the Labour Party was a disgusting hive of anti-Semites, but they were doing their utmost to root out the Nazis, ban all criticism of the IDF, and reverse the mass exodus of Jews from London.[8]

All this was happening in the wake of the notorious Novichok Porridge and Perfume Attacks, allegedly perpetrated by two totally incompetent, pot-smoking, prostitute-banging "assassins" that Putin

5 For a list of these articles, see: https://theguardian.fivefilters.org/antisemitism/)

6 Oppenheim, Maya, "Newsnight denies photoshopping Jeremy Corbyn image to make Labour leader look Russian," The Independent, March 18, 2018

7 Owen Jones on Twitter, March 29, 2018 ("See this? If you're anti Semitic, that's the Labour leadership putting you on notice. So either comprehensively change your outlook or you are going to be kicked out for good." In reference to a Guardian article entitled "John McDonnell says Labour antisemitism will now be eradicated," by Matthew Weaver and Pippa Crerar)

8 Blumenthal, Mandy "'We no longer feel safe in Britain. Anti-Semitism is forcing us to leave our home,'" The Telegraph, July 22, 2018

personally dispatched to Salisbury to miserably fail to take out their target and then waltz around getting photographed by every CCTV camera in Great Britain.[9]

According to the corporate media, Putin tried to cover the crimes of these Jason Bourne-like GRU assassins by ordering his network of Putin-Nazi Twitter bots to flood the Internet with disinformation.[10] Sky News captured and mercilessly interrogated one of these alleged "Twitter bots,"[11] who it turned out was just a feisty British pensioner by the name of Ian ... or at least that's what Putin wants us to believe!

Back in America, millions of liberals and other Russia-and-Trump-obsessives were awaiting the Putin-Nazi Apocalypse, which despite the predictions of Resistance pundits had still, by the Summer, failed to materialize. The corporate media were speculating that Putin's latest "secret scheme" was for Trump to destroy the Atlantic alliance by arriving late for the G7 meeting.

Or maybe Putin's secret scheme was to order Trump to sadistically lock up a bunch of migrants in metal cages, exactly as Obama had done before him[12] ... but these were special Nazi cages! And Trump was separating mothers and children, which, as General Michael Hayden reminded us, was more or less exactly the same as Auschwitz![13]

Paul Krugman had apparently lost it,[14] and was running around the offices of *The New York Times* shrieking that "America as we know it is finished!"

Meanwhile, George Soros had been smuggled back into Europe to single-handedly thwart the Putin-Nazi plot to "dominate the

9 Nicol, Mark, "Novichok suspects' drug-fuelled night of 'cannabis and prostitutes' at £75-a-night East London hotel just hours before Salisbury attack," The Mail on Sunday, September 16, 2018

10 Stewart, Heather, "Russia spread fake news via Twitter bots after Salisbury poisoning," The Guardian, April 19, 2018

11 "Russian 'bot': 'I have no Kremlin contacts'," a television interview with Ian, Sky News, April 20, 2018 ("Here Ian, who has been accused of being a Russian 'bot', says he has no Kremlin contacts.")

12 Mark, Michelle, "Obama officials rushed to explain photos from 2014 that went viral showing locked-up immigrant children — and Trump's facilities look the same," Business Insider, June 19, 2018

13 General Michael Hayden on Twitter, tweeting a photograph of Auschwitz ("Other governments have separated mothers and children")

14 Krugman, Paul, "Trump: A Quisling and His Enablers," The New York Times, June 11, 2018

West," which he planned to do by canceling Brexit (which Putin had obviously orchestrated), and by overthrowing the elected government of Italy (which, according to Soros, was a Putin-Nazi front).[15]

As if that wasn't paranoia-inducing enough, suddenly, Trump flew off to Helsinki to personally meet with the Devil Himself. The neoliberal establishment went totally apeshit. A columnist for *The New York Times* predicted that Trump, Putin, Le Pen, the AfD, and other such Nazis were secretly forming something called "the Alliance of Authoritarian and Reactionary States,"[16] and intended to disband the European Union, and NATO, and impose international martial law and start ethnically cleansing the West of migrants. That, or Trump and Putin were simply using the summit as cover to attend some Nazi-equestrian homosexual orgy, which the *Times* took pains to illustrate by creating a little animated film depicting Trump and Putin as lovers.[17] In any event, Jonathan Chait was certain that Trump had been a "Russian intelligence asset" since at least as early as 1987, and was going to Helsinki to "meet his handler."[18]

In the wake of the summit, the neoliberal Resistance, like some multi-headed mythical creature in the throes of acute amphetamine psychosis, started spastically jabbering about "treason" and "traitors," and more or less demanding that Trump be tried, and taken out and shot on the White House lawn.

A frenzy of neo-McCarthyism followed. Liberals started accusing people of being "traitorous agents of Trump and Moscow,"[19] and openly calling for a CIA coup, because we were "facing a national

---

15 Squires, Nick, "Italy's hard-Right League party angrily dismisses suggestions it is funded by Kremlin," The Telegraph, June 4, 2018 ("Italy's hard-Right League party, part of the new coalition government, has angrily rejected suggestions by the international financier George Soros that it is funded by the Kremlin. At a conference in northern Italy on Sunday, Hungarian-born Mr Soros said he was worried by the close links between The League and Vladimir Putin, the Russian president. 'I don't know if Putin finances the party, but this is a question that Italian public opinion has the right to know,' the billionaire financier was quoted as saying by Italian media.")

16 Cohen, Roger, "Of Course It Could Not Happen Here," The New York Times, June 29, 2018

17 "Trump and Putin - A Love Story," one of a series of three short video cartoons that combine real Donald Trump audio clips with hand-drawn fantasy animations by Bill Plympton, produced by Billy Shebar and David Roberts of 110th Street Films (video available online at https://110th-street.com)

18 Chait, Jonathan, "Will Trump Be Meeting With His Counterpart — Or His Handler?" New York Magazine, July 9, 2018

19 Greenwald, Glenn, "MSNBC Does Not Merely Permit Fabrications Against Democratic Party Critics. It Encourages and Rewards Them," The Intercept, July 8, 2018

security emergency!"[20] A devastating Russian cyber-attack was due to begin at any moment. National Intelligence Director Dan Coats personally assured the *Associated Press* that the little "Imminent Russia Attack" lights he had on his desk were "blinking red."[21]

Into this maelstrom of monomania boldly slunk the Charlottesville Nazis, who had resolved to reenact their infamous national white-supremacist tiki-torch conclave right across the street from the White House this year. The Resistance and Antifa had been promoting this event as the long anticipated Putin-Nazi uprising, and Kristallnacht II, and other such nonsense, so it was a bit of a letdown when only twenty or thirty rather timid Nazis turned up.

It felt like maybe the Great Nazi Panic of 2018 was finally over.

But no, of course it wasn't over. The Nazis had just gone underground. Weeks later, right there on national television, a Jewish-Mexican-American Nazi was spotted transmitting secret Nazi hand signals to her Nazi co-conspirators.[22] One of them, a US Coast Guard member, then relayed the secret Nazi signal to ... well, it wasn't entirely clear, perhaps the Underground Putin-Nazi Navy, which was steaming toward the Florida coast hidden in the eye of Hurricane Florence.[23]

By the Autumn, with the midterm elections fast approaching, the Putin-Nazi terrorists finally struck. It soon became clear that those secret hand signs were just parts of a much larger Trumpian conspiracy to "embolden" a couple of totally psychotic wackos to unleash their hatred on the public. Wacko Number One accomplished this by mailing a series of non-exploding explosive devices to various

20 Frum, David, "The Crisis Facing America," The Atlantic, July 16, 2018 ("America is a very legalistic society, in which public discussion often deteriorates into lawyers arguing about whether any statutes have been violated. But confronting the country in the wake of Helsinki is this question: Can it afford to wait to ascertain why Trump has subordinated himself to Putin after the president has so abjectly demonstrated that he has subordinated himself? Robert Mueller is leading a legal process. The United States faces a national-security emergency.")

21 "Transcript: Dan Coats Warns The Lights Are 'Blinking Red' On Russian Cyberattacks," National Public Radio, July 18, 2018

22 Tacopino, Joe, "Conspiracy about woman at Kavanaugh hearing rages online," New York Post, September 4, 2018 ("A former clerk to Supreme Court nominee Brett Kavanaugh was accused by Twitter trolls of using a 'white supremacist' symbol — even though the woman is of Mexican and Jewish heritage.")

23 Romero, Dennis and Muse, Dystany, "Coast Guard member flashes white power hand signal on TV," NBC News, September 15, 2018

prominent members of the neoliberal Resistance. Wacko Number Two stormed into a synagogue in Pittsburgh and murdered a lot of people.

While the corporate media were unable to prove that Trump, Putin, or possibly Jeremy Corbyn,[24] had personally "emboldened" these wackos, clearly, they had been "emboldened" by somebody, and thus were definitely domestic Putin-Nazi "terrorists," and not just mentally disturbed individuals, like all the other mentally disturbed individuals who go around murdering people all the time.

In November, at last, the tide began to turn. Despite the relentless "chaos campaign to undermine faith in American democracy"[25] that the Russian bots and Nazis were waging, the Democrats managed to win back the House and rescue America from "the brink of fascism."[26] Apparently, the War on Dissent was working, because the millions of Black people that the Russians had brainwashed[27] into not voting for Clinton in 2016 with those Jesus-doesn't-like-masturbation memes[28] had all miraculously been deprogrammed.

Liberals celebrated by singing hymns to Special Prosecutor Robert Mueller[29] and compiling lists of people to subpoena to testify before congressional committees in what will someday be known as "the Hitlergate Hearings."[30] *The New York Times* even published a "roadmap" that Mueller and his team can follow to "send incriminating evidence directly to Congress,"[31] thus protecting this "evidence" from

---

24 Wright, James, "It didn't take a Guardian contributor long to smear Jeremy Corbyn with the Pittsburgh massacre, live on Sky News," The Canary, October 28, 2018 ("During a discussion on a far-right white supremacist massacring 11 people at a Pittsburgh synagogue, writer for the Guardian and Sunday Times, Christina Patterson, accused Corbyn of 'encouraging a climate' of antisemitism.")

25 Barnes, Julian, E. and Rosenberg, Matthew, "Kremlin Sources Go Quiet, Leaving CIA in the Dark About Putin's Plans for Midterms," The New York Times, August 24, 2018

26 Frantz, Douglas, "Is Trump driving the U.S. toward the brink of fascism?" The Globe & Mail, November 1, 2018

27 Shane, Scott and Frenkel, Sheera, "Russian 2016 Influence Operation Targeted African-Americans on Social Media," The New York Times, December 18, 2018

28 Robertson, Adi, "Russian election meddlers started an anti-masturbation hotline, report claims," The Verge, December 17, 2018

29 Upadhyaya, Kayla Kumari, "Women of 'SNL' Sing 'All I Want for Christmas Is You' to Robert Mueller," The Hollywood Reporter, December 1, 2018

30 Hopkins, C. J., "The Hitlergate Hearings," Consent Factory, November 19, 2018

31 Ben-Veniste, Richard and Frampton, George, "Mueller Has a Way Around Trump and His Minions," The New York Times, November 9, 2018

the Justice Department, which is totally infested with Russians and Nazis!

But it's not quite time for liberals to break out the vuvuzelas and Trump effigies yet ... or to ease up on the paranoia. The Putin-Nazi menace is still out there!

The Internet is still literally crawling with all sorts of deviant, division sowing content! And now the Russian bots have brainwashed the French into staging these unruly "Yellow Vest" protests, and the Putin-Nazis have "weaponized" humor,[32] and the economy, and religion, and Brexit, and Wikileaks, and pretty much everything else you can imagine. So this is no time to switch off the television, log off the Internet, and start thinking critically ... or to forget for one moment that THE NAZIS ARE COMING, and that A DEVASTATING RUSSIAN ATTACK IS IMMINENT!

So, here's wishing my Russia-and-Trump-obsessed readers a merry, teeth-clenching, anus-puckering Christmas and a somewhat mentally-healthier New Year!

Me, I'm looking forward to discovering how batshit crazy things can get. I have a feeling we ain't seen nothing yet.

32 *Robinson, Olga, "How Putin's Russia turned humour into a weapon," BBC, December 15, 2018*

The War on Populism

January 10, 2019

Remember when the War on Terror ended and the War on Populism began? That's OK, no one else does.

It happened in the Summer of 2016, also known as "the Summer of Fear."[1] The War on Terror was going splendidly. There had been a series of "terrorist attacks," in Orlando, Nice, Würzberg, Munich, Reutlingen, Ansbach, and Saint-Étienne-du-Rouvray, each of them perpetrated by suddenly "self-radicalized" "lone wolf terrorists" (or "non-terrorist terrorists"[2]) who had absolutely no connection to any type of organized terrorist groups prior to suddenly "self-radicalizing" themselves by consuming "terrorist content" on the Internet. It seemed we were entering a new and even more terrifying phase of the War on Terror, a phase in which anyone could be a "terrorist" and "terrorism" could mean almost anything.

This broadening of the already virtually meaningless definition of "terrorism" was transpiring just in time for Obama to hand off the reins to Hillary Clinton, who everyone knew was going to be the next president, and who was going to have to bomb the crap out of Syria in response to the non-terrorist terrorist threat. The War on Terror (or, rather, "the series of persistent targeted efforts to dismantle specific networks of violent extremists that threaten America," as Obama rebranded it) was going to continue, probably forever. The Brexit referendum had just taken place, but no one had really digested that yet … and then Trump won the nomination.

Like that scene in Orwell's *1984* where the Party switches official enemies right in the middle of the Hate Week rally, the War on Terror was officially canceled and replaced by the War on Populism. Or … all right, it wasn't quite that abrupt. But seriously, go back and scan the news. Note how the "Islamic terrorist threat" we had been

---

1 Connolly, Kate and Willsher, Kim, "Summer of fear: the anxious mood in Germany and France," The Guardian, July 29, 2016

2 Hopkins, C. J., "The Dawning of the Age of Non-Terrorist Terrorism," CounterPunch, August 1, 2016

conditioned to live in fear of on a daily basis since 2001 seemed to just vanish into thin air. Suddenly, the "existential threat" we were facing was "neo-nationalism," "illiberalism," or the pejorative designator du jour, "populism."

Here we are, two and a half years later, and "democracy" is under constant attack by a host of malevolent "populist" forces .... Russo-fascist Black vote suppressors,[3] debaucherous eau de Novichok assassins,[4] Bernie Sanders,[5] the yellow-vested French,[6] emboldened non-exploding mail bomb bombers,[7] Jeremy Corbyn's Nazi Death Cult,[8] and brain-devouring Russian-Cubano crickets.[9] The President of the United States is apparently both a Russian intelligence operative[10] and literally the resurrection of Hitler.[11] NBC and MSNBC have been officially merged with the CIA.[12] *The Guardian* has dispensed with any pretense of journalism and is just making stories up out of whole cloth.[13] Anyone who has ever visited Russia, or met with a Russian, or read a Russian novel, is on an "Enemies of Democracy" watch list, as is anyone refusing to vacation in Israel, which the Senate is now in the process of making mandatory for all

3 Shane, Scott and Frenkel, Sheera, "Russian 2016 Influence Operation Targeted African-Americans on Social Media," The New York Times, December 17, 2018

4 Nicol, Mark, "Novichok suspects' drug-fuelled night of 'cannabis and prostitutes' at £75-a-night East London hotel just hours before Salisbury attack," The Daily Mail, September 16, 2018

5 Brock, David, "Bernie Sanders' fans can't be allowed to poison another Democratic primary with personal attacks," NBC News, January 3, 2019

6 Matlack, Carol and Williams, Robert, "France to Probe Possible Russian Influence on Yellow Vest Riots," Bloomberg News, December 8, 2018

7 Dienst, Jonathan, Winter, Tom, Williams, Pete, and Silva, Daniella, "Some mailed pipe bombs could have been duds, investigators say," NBC News, October 25, 2018 (At least some of the devices found in the wave of suspected pipe bombs mailed to prominent political and media figures had no possibility of exploding ...")

8 Hopkins, C. J., "Jeremy Corbyn's Nazi Death Cult," Consent Factory, April 6, 2018

9 Greenwald, Glenn, "NBC and MSNBC Blamed Russia for Using 'Sophisticated Microwaves' to Cause 'Brain Injuries' in U.S. 'Diplomats' in Cuba. The Culprits Were Likely Crickets." The Intercept, January 7, 2019

10 Chait, Jonathan, "Will Trump Be Meeting With His Counterpart — Or His Handler?" New York Magazine, June 9, 2018

11 Stanley, Jason, "If You're Not Scared About Fascism in the U.S., You Should Be," The New York Times, October 15, 2018

12 Greenwald, Glenn, "Veteran NBC/MSNBC Journalist Blasts the Network for Being Captive to the National Security State and Reflexively Pro-War to Stop Trump," The Intercept, January 3, 2019

13 Greenwald, Glenn, "Five Weeks After The Guardian's Viral Blockbuster Assange-Manafort Scoop, No Evidence Has Emerged — Just Stonewalling," The Intercept, January 2, 2019

US citizens.[14] Meanwhile, the "terrorists" are nowhere to be found, except for the terrorists we've been using[15] to attempt to overthrow the government of Bashar al Assad, the sadistic non-nerve-gassing Monster of Syria,[16] who illegally invaded and conquered his own country in defiance of the "international community."

All this madness has something to do with "populism," although it isn't clear what. The leading theory is that the Russians are behind it. They've got some sort of hypno-technology (not to be confused with those brain-eating crickets) capable of manipulating the minds of ... well, Black people, mostly,[17] but not just Black people. Obviously, they are also controlling the French, who they have transformed into "racist, hate-filled liars"[18] who are "attacking elected representatives, journalists, Jews, foreigners, and homosexuals," according to French President Emmanuel Macron, the anointed "Golden Boy of Europe."[19]

More terrifying still, Putin is now able to project words out of Trump's mouth in real time, literally using Trump's head as a puppet, or like one of those Mission Impossible masks. Rachel Maddow conclusively proved this by spending a couple of hours on Google comparing the words coming out of Trump's mouth to words that had come out of Russian mouths, but that had never come out of American mouths, which, they turned out to be the exact same words, or pretty close to the exact same words![20] Apparently, Putin's master plan for Total Populist World Domination and Establishment of the

14 Grim, Ryan and Greenwald, Glenn, "U.S. Senate's First Bill, in the Midst of the Shutdown, Is a Bipartisan Defense of the Israeli Government From Boycotts," The Intercept, January 5, 2019

15 Carden, James, "Why Does the US Continue to Arm Terrorists in Syria?" The Nation, March 3, 2017

16 "Syria war: What we know about Douma 'chemical attack'," BBC News, July 10, 2018 ("On 6 July, a preliminary report issued by the OPCW said 'no organophosphorus nerve agents or their degradation products were detected, either in the environmental samples or in plasma samples from the alleged casualties'".)

17 Love, David A., "Russia's targeting of black voters is a very American thing to do," CNN, December 20, 2018

18 Sage, Adam, "Gilets jaunes are violent, racist, hate-filled liars, says Macron," The Times, January 1, 2019

19 Chrisafis, Angelique, "Macron's appeal to French from behind gold desk leaves gilets jaunes unimpressed," The Guardian, December 11, 2018

20 Maddow, Rachel, "Trump curiously well versed in specific Russian talking points," MSNBC, January 4, 2019

Thousand Year Duginist Reich was to provoke the global capitalist ruling classes, the corporate media, and their credulous disciples into devolving into stark raving lunatics, or blithering idiots, or a combination of both.

But, seriously, all that actually happened back in the Summer of 2016 was the global capitalist ruling classes recognized that they had a problem. The problem that they recognized they had (and continue to have, and are now acutely aware of) is that no one is enjoying global capitalism … except the global capitalist ruling classes.

The whole smiley-happy, supranational, neo-feudal corporate empire concept is not going over very well with the masses, or at least not with the unwashed masses. People started voting for right-wing parties, and Brexit, and other "populist" measures, not because they had suddenly transformed into Nazis, but because the Right was acknowledging and exploiting their anger with the advance of global neoliberalism, while liberals and the Identity Politics Left were slow jamming the TPP with Obama[21] and babbling about transgender bathrooms, and such.

The global capitalist ruling classes needed to put a stop to that (i.e, the "populist" revolt, not the bathroom debate). So they suspended the Global War on Terror and launched the War on Populism. It was originally only meant to last until Hillary Clinton's coronation, or the second Brexit referendum, then switch back to the War on Terror, but … well, weird things happen, and here we are.

We'll get back to the War on Terror, eventually. The War on Populism is essentially just a temporary rebranding of it. In the end, it's all the same counter-insurgency.

When a system is globally hegemonic, as our current model of capitalism is, *every "war" is a counter-insurgency*, a war waged against an internal enemy, as there are no external enemies to fight. The character of these internal enemies might change (e.g., "Islamic terrorism," "extremism," "fascism," "populism," "Trumpism," "Corbynism," et cetera) but they are all insurgencies against the hegemonic system … which, in our case, is global capitalism, *not* the United States of America.

---

21 Zillman, Claire, "Watch President Obama 'Slow Jam' His Economic Record With Jimmy Fallon," Fortune, June 10, 2016

The way I see it, the global capitalist ruling classes now have less than two years to put down this current "populist" insurgency.

First and foremost, they need to get rid of Trump, who, despite his bombastic nativist rhetoric, is clearly no "hero of the common man," nor any threat to global capitalism, but who has become an anti-establishment symbol, like a walking, talking "fuck you" to both the American and global neoliberal elites.

Then, they need to get a handle on Europe, which isn't going to be particularly easy. What happens next in France will be telling, as will whatever becomes of Brexit (which I continue to believe will never actually happen, except perhaps in some purely nominal sense).

And then there's the battle for hearts and minds, which they've been furiously waging for the last two years, and which is only going to intensify. If you think things are batshit crazy now (which, clearly, they are), strap yourself in. What is coming is going to make COINTELPRO look like the work of some amateur meme-freak.

The neoliberal corporate media, psy-ops like Integrity Initiative,[22] Internet-censoring apps like NewsGuard, ShareBlue and other David Brock outfits,[23] and a legion of mass hysteria generators[24] will be relentlessly barraging our brains with absurdity, disinformation, and just outright lies (as will their counterparts on the Right, of course, in case you thought that they were any alternative).

It's going to get extremely zany.

The good news is, by the time it's all over, and Donald Trump has been dealt with, and normality restored, and the working classes put back in their places, we probably won't remember that any of this

---

22 Blumenthal, Max and Ames, Mark, "Covert British military-intelligence smear machine is meddling in American politics, documents reveal," The Grayzone, January 8, 2019 ("The Integrity Initiative has mobilized an international disinformation campaign across Europe. Now, with government and right-wing foundation money, this massive "political smear unit" is infiltrating the US.")

23 Borosage, Robert L., "The Poisonous Politics of David Brock," The Nation, January 19, 2017

24 Coppins, McKay, "How the Left Lost Its Mind," The Atlantic, July 2, 2017 ("The Trump era has given rise to a vast alternative left-wing media infrastructure that operates largely out of the view of casual news consumers, but commands a massive audience and growing influence in liberal America. There are polemical podcasters and partisan click farms; wild-eyed conspiracists and cynical fabulists. Some traffic heavily in rumor and wage campaigns of misinformation; others are merely aggregators and commentators who have carved out a corner of the web for themselves. But taken together, they form a media universe where partisan hysteria is too easily stoked, and fake news can travel at the speed of light.")

happened. We'll finally be able to sort out those bathrooms, and get back to paying the interest on our debts, and to living in more or less constant fear of an imminent devastating terrorist attack … and won't that be an enormous relief?

The Magic Socialist

February 25, 2019

So here it is, the announcement we've been waiting for … all aboard for another cruise on the new and improved USS Magic Socialist with your captain Bernie Sanders at the helm! If you're not familiar with this extraordinary vessel, it's like the luxury liner in *The Magic Christian*,[1] except catering to credulous American socialists instead of the British filthy rich. Tickets start at just $27 dollars … so hurry, because they're going fast!

That's right, folks, Bernie is back, and this time it's not just a sadistic prank where he gets you all fired up about his fake "revolution" for fifteen months, gets cheated out of the nomination, then backs whichever corporate-bought candidate the Democratic Party orders you to vote for.

No, this time the Bernster really means it! This time, when the DNC rigs the primaries to hand the nomination to Harris, or Biden, or some billionaire android like Michael Bloomberg, Bernie is not going to break your heart by refusing to run as an independent candidate, completely unbeholden to the corporations and oligarchs that own both political parties, or otherwise make you feel like a sucker for buying his "revolution" schtick. He's not going to fold like a fifty-dollar suit and start parroting whatever propaganda the corporate media will be prodigiously spewing to convince you that the Russians and Nazis are coming unless you vote for the empire's pre-anointed puppet!

Bernie would never dream of doing that … or at least he'd never dream of doing that twice.

There are limits, after all, to people's gullibility. It's not like you can just run the same con, with the same fake message and the same fake messiah, over and over, and expect folks to fall for it. If you could, well, that would be extremely depressing. That would mean you could get folks to believe almost anything, or that we were stuck in some eter-

---

1 The Magic Christian, 1969 Film, based on the novel by Terry Southern

nally recurring multi-dimensional reality loop. The next year and a half in American politics would play out like one of those *Groundhog Day* knock-offs meets *The Magic Christian* meets *The Usual Suspects*, directed by David Lynch, on acid. We'd be barraged by recycled Feel-the-Bern memes. Hacky sack shares would go through the roof. That creepy little bird would come fluttering back, land on Bernie's podium again, and chirp out "L'Internationale." People would start booking Tim Robbins for interviews. Ben & Jerry's would roll out another revolutionary flavor of Bernie ice cream … and in the end it would all amount to nothing.

But that's not going to happen this time. No, this time, the USS Magic Socialist is setting sail straight for Socialismland! This time, it's really the Revolution! The end of global capitalism! And the best part of the whole deal is, you don't even have to take up arms, stage a series of wildcat strikes, blockade major highways, occupy airports, or otherwise cripple the US economy … all you have to do is vote for Bernie!

See, that's the magic of electoral politics! The global capitalist ruling establishment, despite the fact that they own the banks and the corporations that own the government that owns the military and Intelligence services, and despite the fact that they own the media, and all essential industries, and channels of trade, and are relentlessly restructuring the entire planet (which they rule with almost total impunity) to conform to their soulless neoliberal ideology, and are more than happy to unleash their militarized goons on anyone who gets in their way[2] … despite all that, if we elect Bernie president, they will have no choice but to peacefully surrender, and transform America into a socialist wonderland!

Sure, they won't be happy about it, but they will have no choice but to go along with whatever Bernie and his followers want, because that's how American democracy works!

We've seen it in action these last two years, since Donald Trump got elected president. The establishment wasn't too thrilled about that, but they had to put aside their own selfish interests and respect

---

2 Bock, Pauline, "The French police's brutality against the gilets jaunes can no longer be denied," New Statesman, January 30, 2019 ("A video of pacifist protester Jérôme Rodrigues being blinded in one eye has come to symbolise the state's intolerance of dissent.")

the will of the American people … because imagine what might have happened if they hadn't!

For example, they might have concocted a story about Trump being a Russian intelligence asset who was personally conspiring with Vladimir Putin[3] to destroy the fabric of Western democracy so that Russia could take over the entire planet.[4] They could have had respected newspapers like *The New York Times* and *The Washington Post* and television networks like CNN and MSNBC disseminate this story, and subtly reinforce it in endless variations, on a daily basis for over two years. They could have appointed a special prosecutor to investigate the facts of their made-up story, and indict a bunch of unextraditable Russians and a handful of inveterate DC slimebags to make the whole thing look legitimate. At the same time, they could have had the media warn everybody, over and over, that Trump, in addition to being a traitor, was also the second coming of Hitler,[5] and was on the verge of torching the Capitol,[6] declaring himself Führer, and rounding up the Jews. They could have generated so much mass hysteria and Putin-Nazi paranoia that liberals would literally be seeing Russians and Nazis coming out of the woodwork!

Fortunately, the global capitalist establishment, out of respect for democracy and the American people, decided not to go that route. If Americans chose to elect a jabbering imbecile president, that was their right, and far be it from the empire to interfere. Tempting as it must have been to use all their power to demonize Trump in order to teach the world what happens when you get elected president without their permission, they restrained themselves … and thank God for that! I don't even want to contemplate the extent of the rage and cynicism they would have fomented among the public by doing those things I just outlined above. That might have left people with the false impression that their votes mean absolutely nothing, and that the entire US electoral system is just a simulation of democra-

---

3 Chait, Jonathan, "Will Trump Be Meeting With His Counterpart — Or His Handler?" New York Magazine, July 9, 2018

4 Cohen, Roger, "Of Course It Could Not Happen Here," The New York Times, June 29, 2018

5 "If you're not scared about fascism in the U.S., you should be," The New York Times, October 15, 2018 (A video by Jason Stanley)

6 Adams, Becket, "Washington Post columnist: I'm not saying Trump is Hitler, but this migrant caravan stuff is like the Reichstag fire," Washington Examiner, October 26, 2018

cy, and, in reality, they are living in a neo-feudalist, de facto global capitalist empire administrated by omnicidal money-worshipping human parasites that won't be satisfied until they've remade the whole of creation in their nihilistic image.

Thankfully, the ruling classes spared us all that, so now we can hop aboard the Magic Socialist and take another cruise with Cap'n Bernie! Considering how magnanimous they've been with Trump, once Bernie wins the election fair and square, the empire clearly won't have any problems with him nationalizing the US healthcare system, tripling taxes on the super-rich, subsidizing university education, and all that other cool socialism stuff (i.e., the stuff we mostly still have here in Europe, along with some semblance of cultural solidarity, although the global capitalists are working to fix that).

Oh, and in case you're worried about Bernie backing the empire's ongoing regime-change op in Venezuela, don't be. He's just playing 4D chess, like Obama did throughout his presidency, by pretending to do the empire's bidding while he actually went about the business of resurrecting hope and eradicating racism. Bernie's just being sly like that! It might seem like he's aligning himself with mass murdering thugs like Elliot Abrams and sadistic ass freaks like Marco Rubio,[7] but he isn't. Not really. It's just an act. I mean, he has to get elected, doesn't he?

How else are we going to get to Socialismland?

---

7 Johnstone, Caitlin, "Psychopathic US Senator Openly Calls For Maduro To Suffer Gaddafi's Fate," Medium, February 24, 2019

Anti-Semitism Pandemic

March 11, 2019

Get the kids into the house! Lock your doors! Board up the windows! Break out the gas masks and hazmat suits! According to the corporate media, we are now officially deep in the throes of a deadly anti-Semitism pandemic!

And just as the threat of mind-controlling Russian influencers was finally waning! It appears the fabric of Western democracy just can't catch a break these days.

The origins of this pernicious, panic-inducing pestilence remain, for the most part, shrouded in mystery, but epidemiologists now believe that it began in the Spring of 2015, shortly after the resignation of Ed Milliband as UK Labour Party leader, and went global in the Summer of 2016, right around the time of the Brexit referendum and the nomination of Donald Trump. (Although the circumstantial evidence is overwhelming, to date, there exists no conclusive proof that Russian bio-weapons designers cooked up the virus in a hotel in Salisbury and sprayed it onto anyone's doorknob.)

Virologists are working around the clock to map the genome of this scurrilous scourge, about which very little is known, other than that it has a sudden onset, and attacks the language center of the brain, causing the sufferer to express opinions about "Zionism," "globalism," "the Israel lobby," "banks," and other code words for "Jews." Patients appear to be unaware that they are spouting these anti-Semitic code words until they are told they are by the corporate media, or by their colleagues, or some random account on Twitter, at which point their symptoms alter dramatically, and they suffer a series of petit mal seizures, causing them to repeatedly publicly apologize for unintentionally advocating the extermination of the entire Jewish people and the establishment of a worldwide Nazi Reich.

At the moment, Britain is taking the brunt of it. Despite the best efforts of the ruling classes and the media to contain its spread, several new cases of anti-Semitism have been reported throughout the Kingdom, or at least among the Labour Party, which, at this point, has been so thoroughly infected that it resembles a neo-Nazi death cult.[1]

Jeremy Corbyn, who contracted the virus more or less the moment he assumed the leadership, is now exhibiting symptoms of late-stage disease. Reliable sources close to the party, reached for comment at a brunch in Qatar with Tony Blair and a bunch of Saudis, report that Corbyn is running around Momentum HQ in full Nazi regalia, alternately heiling Hitler and looking for journalists to apologize to.

Another Labour MP, Chris Williamson, had to be summarily quarantined after publicly apologizing for not apologizing for inciting a gathering of Labour members to stop apologizing for refusing to apologize for being disgusting anti-Semites … or something basically along those lines.

Owen Jones is fiercely denying denying that the party is a hive of disgusting Nazis, and that he ever denied that denying the fact that there is zero actual evidence of that fact[2] is essential to preserving what is left of the party, once it has been cured of anti-Semitism, or disbanded and reconstituted from scratch.

Emergency measures are now in effect. A full-scale Labour Party lockdown is imminent. Anyone not already infected is being advised to flee the party, denounce anyone who hasn't done so as "a Hitler-loving Corbyn-sympathizer," and prophylactically apologize for any critical statements they might have made about Israel, or "elites," or "global capitalism," or "bankers," or anything else that anyone can construe as anti-Semitism (preferably in the pages of *The Guardian*[3]).

Nor has the Continent been spared!

What at first appeared to be a series of spontaneous protests against Emmanuel Macron, economic austerity, and global capital-

---

1 Cohen, Roger, "Jeremy Corbyn's Anti-Semitic Labour Party," The New York Times, February 28, 2019

2 Knightly, Kit, "Anti-Capitalism is NOT Anti-Semitism," OffGuardian, March 5, 2019 (Including pie charts from a study by the Institute for Jewish Policy Research indicating that, as of March 2019, cases of anti-Semitism in the Labour Party amounted to 0.08 percent of the membership.)

3 Harris, John, "The unanswered question: why do antisemites think Labour is the party for them?" the Guardian, March 4, 2019

ism by the so-called "Yellow Vests" in France has now been officially diagnosed as a nationwide anti-Semitism outbreak.[4]

In a heroic attempt to contain the outbreak, Macron has dispatched his security forces to shoot the eyes out of unarmed women,[5] pepper spray paraplegics in wheelchairs,[6] and just generally beat bloody hell out of everyone.[7]

Strangely, none of these tactics have worked, so France has decided to join the US, the UK, Germany, and the rest of the empire in defining anti-Zionism as form of anti-Semitism,[8] such that anyone implying that Israel is, in any way, inherently racist, or a quasi-fascist Apartheid state, or making jokes about "elites" or "bankers," can be detained and prosecuted for committing a "hate-crime."

Meanwhile, in the United States (where Donald Trump, i.e., "US patient zero," had already single-handedly infected the vast majority of the American populace, and transformed the nation into an unrecognizable, genocidal Nazi Reich), the anti-Semitism virus has now spread to Congress, where Representative Ilhan Omar (reputed to be a hardcore member of the infamous "Axis of Anti-Semitism"[9]) has apparently totally lost her mind and started talking about the Israel lobby, and the billions of dollars that the US government provides to Israel on an annual basis, and other Israel-related subjects one simply does not talk about ... unless one writes for *The New York Times* and isn't a hijab-wearing Muslim, in which case it's completely fine to characterize support for Israel as being "bought and paid for by the Israel lobby."[10]

---

4 Vandoorne, Saskya, "Yellow Vest protesters fan flames of anti-Semitism in France," CNN, March 9, 2019

5 "'I do not recognize my country': Yellow Vests who have lost eyes, limbs demand justice from Macron," RT, February 16, 2019

6 "Disabled Yellow Vest pepper sprayed by French Police in Paris" (Video), The Sun, March 4, 2019

7 Bock, Pauline, "The French police's brutality against the gilets jaunes can no longer be denied," New Statesman, January 30, 2019

8 Lough, Richard, "France's Macron says anti-Zionism is a form of anti-Semitism," Reuters, February 21, 2019

9 Kerstein, Benjamin, "Ilhan Omar and the Axis of Antisemitism," The Algemeiner, March 10, 2019

10 Friedman, Thomas L., "Newt, Mitt, Bibi and Vladimir," The New York Times, December 13, 2011 ("I sure hope that Israel's prime minister, Benjamin Netanyahu, understands that the standing ovation he got in Congress this year was not for his politics. That ovation was bought and paid for by the Israel lobby.")

Now, this is where things get really confusing. Trump (who, let's remember, is Literally Hitler, or was until he green-lit the attempted US coup in Venezuela) and the Republicans have now united with the Democrats to denounce Ilhan Omar as a filthy anti-Semite, and possibly a full-fledged Islamic terrorist (or to condemn the existence of "hate," or something). The corporate media, Facebook, and Twitter have been overtaken by hordes of angry anti-Semites accusing other anti-Semites of anti-Semitism. Congress is on the verge of convening a House Un-Israeli Activities Committee to investigate anyone who might have ever trafficked in "anti-Semitic tropes." Meghan McCain was so thoroughly horrified by the hateful, anti-Semitic things that Ilhan Omar never said that she broke down blubbering on national television and begged Joy Behar to call in a Rabbi to convert her to Judaism on the spot, which some viewers found a bit unseemly.[11]

OK, I know, you're probably questioning the fact that this alleged anti-Semitism pandemic just sprang up out of the ether one day, more or less in perfect sync with the Russian plot to destroy democracy that Vladimir Putin set in motion the moment the Global War on Terror seemed to be running out of steam. If you are, you need to close this essay, pull up either MSNBC or *The Guardian* website on your phone, and inoculate yourself against such thoughts. That conspiratorial type of thinking is one of the early warning signs that you have been infected with anti-Semitism! Unless you act now to protect yourself, before you know it, you'll be raving about "the ruling classes," "globalist elites," "austerity," "neoliberalism," "the Israel lobby," or even "Palestinians."

So just put all that stuff out of your mind! This sudden anti-Semitism outbreak has nothing to do with the War on Populism that the global capitalist ruling classes have been waging for the last two years. It's not like the establishment would stoop so low as to use anti-Semitism (and even the Holocaust!) as a cynical propaganda ploy to delegitimize their myriad opponents and critics.

---

11 Staff, Toi and Agencies, "Meghan McCain raps anti-Semitism, gets 'anti-Semitic' treatment by Jewish artist," Times of Israel, March 10, 2019 ("Emotional criticism by Meghan McCain of Democrat Congresswoman Ilhan Omar's allegedly anti-Semitic remarks has spawned an online uproar, after [Eli Valley] a Jewish artist drew a cartoon that mocked the late Arizona senator's daughter and was himself accused of employing anti-Semitic tropes and imagery.")

No, it's much more believable that an idiopathic, worldwide anti-Semitism pandemic erupted, for no apparent reason, precisely as the capitalist ruling classes were beginning to suspect that they had a widespread "populist" insurgency on their hands.

Plus, even if our democratic leaders and the professional journalists in the corporate media were, in fact, a bunch of soulless, conniving, sociopathic scumbags, what purpose would it possibly serve for them to whip the public up into a series of fits of mass hysteria over anti-Semitism, or "populism," or imaginary Russian hackers, or imminent lone-wolf terrorist attacks, possibly with homemade nuclear devices?

That wouldn't make any sense, now would it? People would be so consumed with fear and hatred that they could hardly think. They might not even notice how they were being cynically manipulated, and were contributing to actual anti-Semitism[12] by rendering the term devoid of any meaning.

No, the idiopathic anti-Semitism pandemic theory makes a lot more sense. So get out those vintage plague doctor masks, lock your critical thinking up in your anti-anti-Semitism safe room, and pull up *Schindler's List* on Netflix … oh, and don't forget to scour the Internet for any criticism of the capitalist ruling classes, or the corporate media, or neoliberalism, or any other anti-Semitic tropes![13]

12 Medem, Mendi, "Philosemitism is the New Antisemitism: How Jews Are (Still) Used to Manage Exploitation," Jewdas, October 15, 2018

13 David Schneider on Twitter, March 8, 2019 ("This shocks me: 'certain dark forces are using their power and contacts in the media to undermine this project.' If you/Williamson didn't know this is an antisemitic trope going back centuries then education is needed. If you/he did know, it's antisemitism.")

Mueller-Dämmerung

March 21, 2019

If Nietzsche was right, and what doesn't kill us makes us stronger, we can thank the global capitalist ruling classes, the Democratic Party, and the corporate media for four more years of Donald Trump.

The long-awaited Mueller report is due any day now, or so they keep telling us. Once it is delivered, and does not prove that Trump is a Russian intelligence asset, or that he personally conspired with Vladimir Putin to steal the presidency from Hillary Clinton ... well, things are liable to get a bit awkward. Given the amount of goal-post-moving and focus-shifting that has been going on, clearly, this is what everyone's expecting.

Honestly, I'm a bit surprised. I was sure they were going to go ahead and fabricate some kind of "smoking gun" evidence (like the pee-stained sheets from that Moscow hotel), or coerce one of his sleazy minions into testifying that he personally saw Trump down on his knees "colluding" Putin in the back room of a Russian sauna. After all, if you're going to accuse a president of being a "Russian Intelligence asset," you kind of need to be able to prove it, or (a) you defeat the whole purpose of the exercise, (b) you destroy your own credibility, and (c) you present that president with a powerful weapon he can use to bury you.

This is not exactly rocket science. As any seasoned badass will tell you, when you're resolving a conflict with another seasoned badass, you don't take out a gun unless you're going to use it. Taking a gun out, waving it around, and not shooting the other badass with it, is generally not a winning strategy. What often happens, if you're dumb enough to do that, is that the other badass will take your gun from you and either shoot you or beat you senseless with it.

This is what Trump is about to do with Russiagate. When the Mueller report fails to present any evidence that he "colluded" with Russia to steal the election, Trump is going to reach over, grab that report, roll it up tightly into a makeshift cudgel, and then beat the snot out of his opponents with it. He is going to explain to the American people that the Democrats, the corporate media, Hollywood, the liberal intelligentsia, and elements of the U.S. Intelligence agencies conspired to try to force him out of office with an unprecedented propaganda campaign and a groundless special investigation.[1] He is going to explain to the American people that Russiagate, from start to finish, was, in his words, a ridiculous "witch hunt," a childish story based on nothing. Then he's going to tell them a different story.

That story goes a little something like this ...

Back in November of 2016, the American people were so fed up with the neoliberal oligarchy that everyone knows really runs the country that they actually elected Donald Trump president. They did this fully aware that Trump was a repulsive, narcissistic ass clown who bragged about "grabbing women by the pussy" and jabbered about building "a big, beautiful wall" and making the Mexican government pay for it. They did this fully aware of the fact that Donald Trump had zero experience in any political office whatsoever, was a loudmouth bigot, and was possibly out of his gourd on amphetamines half the time.

The American people did not care. They were so disgusted with being conned by arrogant, two-faced, establishment stooges like the Clintons, the Bushes, and Barack Obama, that they chose to put Donald Trump in office, because, fuck it, what did they have to lose?

The oligarchy that runs the country responded to the American people's decision by inventing a completely cock-and-bull story about Donald Trump being a Russian agent who the American people were tricked into voting for by nefarious Russian mind-control operatives, getting every organ of the liberal corporate media to disseminate and relentlessly promote this story on a daily basis for nearly three years, and appointing a special prosecutor to conduct an official investigation in order to lend it the appearance of legitimacy.

Every component of the ruling establishment (i.e., the government, the media, the Intelligence agencies, the liberal intelligentsia, et al.) collaborated in an unprecedented effort to remove an American president from office based on a bunch of made-up horseshit, which kind of amounts to an attempted soft coup.

1 Doran, Michael, "The Real Collusion Story," National Review, March 13, 2019

This is the story that Donald Trump is going to tell the American people.

A minority of ideological heretics on what passes for the American Left are going to help him tell this story, not because we support Donald Trump, but because we believe that the mass hysteria and authoritarian fanaticism that has been manufactured over the course of Russiagate represents a danger greater than Trump.

It has reached some neo-Riefenstahlian level, this bug-eyed, spittle-flecked, cult-like behavior, worse even than the manufactured mass hysteria that gripped most Americans back in 2003, when they cheered on the U.S. invasion of Iraq, and the murder, rape, and torture of hundreds of thousands of men, women, and children based on a bunch of made-up horseshit.

We are going to be vilified, we leftist heretics, for helping Trump tell Americans this story. We are going to be denounced as "Trumpenleft traitors," "Putin-sympathizers," and "Nazi-adjacents" (as we were denounced as "terrorist-sympathizers" and "Saddam-loving traitors" back in 2003). We are going to be denounced as all these things by liberals, and by other leftists. We are going to be warned that pointing out how the government, the media, and the Intelligence agencies all worked together to sell people Russiagate will only get Trump reelected, and, if that happens, it will be the End of Everything.

It will not be the End of Everything.

What might, however, be the End of Everything, or might lead us down the road to the End of Everything, is if otherwise intelligent human beings continue to allow themselves to be whipped into fits of mass hysteria and run around behaving like a mindless herd of propaganda-regurgitating zombies whenever the global capitalist ruling classes tell them that "the Russians are coming!" or that "the Nazis are coming!" or that "the Terrorists are coming!"

The Russo-Nazi Terrorists are not coming. The global capitalist ruling classes are putting down a populist insurgency, delegitimizing any and all forms of dissent from their global capitalist ideology and resistance to the hegemony of global capitalism. In the process, they are conditioning people to completely abandon their critical faculties and behave like twitching Pavlovian idiots who will obediently respond to whatever stimuli or blatantly fabricated propaganda the corporate media bombards them with.

If you want a glimpse of the dystopian future, it isn't an Orwellian boot in your face. It's *Invasion of the Body Snatchers*.

Study the Russiagate believers' reactions to the Mueller report when it is finally delivered. Observe the bizarre intellectual contortions their minds perform to attempt to rationalize their behavior over the last three years.

Trust me, it will not be pretty. Cognitive dissonance never is.

Or, who knows, maybe the Russiagate gang will pull a fast one at the eleventh hour, and accuse Robert Mueller of Putinist sympathies (or appearing in that FSB video of Trump's notorious Moscow pee-party), and appoint a special prosecutor to investigate the special prosecutor. That should get them through to 2020!

A Russiagate Requiem

April 2, 2019

So the Mueller report is finally in, and it appears that hundreds of millions of Americans have, once again, been woefully bamboozled.

Weird, how this just keeps on happening.

At this point, Americans have to be the most frequently woefully bamboozled people in the entire history of woeful bamboozlement.

If you didn't know better, you'd think we were all a bunch of hopelessly credulous imbeciles that you could con into believing almost anything, or that our brains had been bombarded with so much official propaganda from the time we were born that we couldn't really even think anymore.

That's right, as I'm sure you're aware by now, it turns out President Donald Trump, the pompous former reality TV star who can barely string three sentences together without totally losing his train of thought and barking like an elephant seal, is not, in fact, a secret agent conspiring with the Russian Intelligence services to destroy the fabric of Western democracy.

After two long years of bug-eyed hysteria, Inspector Mueller came up with squat. Zip. Zero. Nichts. Nada. Or, all right, he indicted a bunch of Russians that will never see the inside of a courtroom, and a few of Trump's professional sleazebags for lying and assorted other sleazebag activities … so, I guess that was worth the $25 million of taxpayers' money that was spent on this circus.

Notwithstanding those historic accomplishments, the entire Mueller investigation now appears to have been another wild goose chase, like the "search" for those non-existent WMDs that we invaded and destabilized the Middle East and murdered hundreds of thousands of people pretending to conduct in 2003. Paranoid collusion-obsessives will continue to obsess about redactions and cover-ups,[1] but the long and short of the matter is, there will be no

---

1 Hains, Tim, "MSNBC's Joy Reid on Mueller Report: It Feels Like The Seeds Of A Cover-Up Are Here," Real Clear Politics, March 24, 2019

perp walks for any of the Trumps. No treason tribunals. No televised hangings. No detachment of Secret Service agents marching Hillary into the White House.

The jig, as they say, is up.

But let's try to look on the bright side, shall we? Disgraceful as this Russiagate fiasco has been, at least it was all just an honest mistake, and not any kind of plot, or conspiracy, or anything as disturbing as that. It's not like the majority of the corporate media perpetrated a massive, coordinated, Intelligence agency-initiated psyop on the Western public for two and half years. No, they just "got it wrong," again ... like they did with those Iraqi WMDs.

The corporate media, after all, are comprised of dedicated, professional journalists, who maintain the highest ethical standards, and who would never knowingly bombard the masses with hysterical McCarthyite propaganda based on absolutely nothing but the word of a bunch of deep-state types who were trying to force a president out of office and delegitimize a populist backlash against the spread of global neoliberalism.

Plus, there is no "deep state." Not really. That's just one of those right-wing conspiracy theories that only Trump-loving fascists believe in. I mean, it's not as if elements of the FBI, the DOJ, and the DNC paid a former MI6 spook working for a Washington PR firm contracted by a Washington law firm contracted by the Clinton campaign to fabricate a "dossier" alleging that "the Russian regime [sic] has been cultivating, supporting, and assisting Trump for at least five years" in order "to sow discord" within the Transatlantic Alliance, and then fed that fabricated dossier to their contacts in the corporate media, who used it to generate mass hysteria, which the Congress then used to justify the appointment of a special prosecutor, whose investigation of the allegations contained in the fabricated dossier the corporate media and deep-state types used to generate even more mass hysteria ... and so on, until hundreds of millions of people actually believed that Donald Trump was some kind of Russian Intelligence asset, and was going to be impeached and tried for treason.

Now, that would be scary, if that had happened!

Another thing that (thank Christ!) didn't happen was when the corporate media hired a bunch of ex-Intelligence agency officials to appear on their "news" shows every other night disseminating Russiagate propaganda, while at the same time effectively banning journalists with dissenting views from challenging their lies. Or … OK, to the degree they did that (and they certainly did it to some degree), they didn't do it intentionally, or knowingly, or with malice aforethought or criminal intent. They probably just misplaced the telephone numbers (and the email addresses and Twitter handles) of Matt Taibbi, Glenn Greenwald, Aaron Maté, and other infamous "collusion rejectionists,"2 so they had no choice but to bring in the spooks.

Look, I don't want to beat this to death. The important thing is that we can all be grateful that none of that stuff I just mentioned happened, and, basically, just shut up and get back to work. This is not the time to remind everybody how totally insane and hysterical things got, and how they ran around like headless chickens[3] squawking about "Russians" coming out of the woodwork, accusing anyone they disagreed with of being "Kremlin agents" or "Russian bots," and begging corporations to censor the Internet.

No, it's time to, you know, let bygones be bygones, and just forget about all this "Russiagate" business, and the FBI, and that made-up dossier, and how respected publications like *The Washington Post*, *The New York Times*, *The Guardian*, and others published completely fabricated stories about secret meetings that never took place,[4] power grid hackings that never happened,[5] Russia-linked servers that never existed,[6] imaginary Russian propaganda peddlers,[7] and … well, too many other examples to list.

Talking about all that is just a distraction, as my former colleagues on what has recently become the radical Rooskie-hunting Left

2 *"Watch Aaron Maté Destroy Russiagate Propagandist and 'Collusion' Author Luke Harding," (Video), Foreign Policy Journal, October 6, 2018*

3 *Hopkins, C. J., "The Year of the Headless Liberal Chicken," Consent Factory, December 8, 2017*

4 *Greenwald, Glenn, "Five Weeks After The Guardian's Viral Blockbuster Assange-Manafort Scoop, No Evidence Has Emerged — Just Stonewalling," The Intercept, January 2, 2019*

5 *Eilperin, Juliet and Entous, Adam, "Russian operation hacked a Vermont utility, showing risk to U.S. electrical grid security, officials say," The Washington Post, December 30, 2016*

6 *Foer, Franklin, "Was a Trump Server Communicating With Russia?" Slate, October 31, 2016*

7 *Timberg, Craig, "Russian propaganda effort helped spread fake news during election, experts say," The Washington Post, November 24, 2016*

wasted no time in advising everyone.[8] Worse, it only helps Donald Trump, who, OK, maybe isn't a Russian Intelligence asset anymore, but is still almost literally Adolf Hitler … or at least some sort of inhuman monster that bears no resemblance whatsoever to Obama or any other normal president, and who is certainly going to declare martial law, proclaim himself Führer, and unleash his underground white supremacist army on us, or something more or less along those lines.

And as for the non-existent deep state, and the Democrats, and the corporate media, and the millions of Americans they accidentally bamboozled … well, I imagine they're feeling pretty silly right now. So, this is not the time to demand a full accounting from the patriots in the Intelligence community, or to compare the professionals in the corporate media to the keys of an enormous Goebbelsian piano mechanically hammering out whatever tune the ruling classes decide to play.

Yes, they made a few mistakes, and got a little carried away, but they're only human, after all. I'm sure they're all very, very sorry, and will never, ever, do it again.

---

8 CounterPunch editor Joshua Frank on Twitter, March 30, 2019 ("Five domestic issues more important than the Mueller report: 1) Immigrants being held under a Texas overpass. 2) Trump's revival of Keystone XL. 3) 6-week abortion ban to be signed into Georgia law. 4) Yellowstone Bison are being slaughtered. 5) Rolling Stones postpone US tour!")

Democracy vs. the Putin-Nazis

May 23, 2019

Back in January 2018, I wrote about The War on Dissent,[1] which, in case you haven't noticed, is going gangbusters. As predicted, the global capitalist ruling classes have been using every weapon in their arsenal to marginalize, stigmatize, delegitimize, and otherwise eliminate any and all forms of dissent from neoliberal ideology, and in particular from their new official narrative ... "Democracy versus The Putin-Nazis."

For over two years, the corporate media have been pounding out an endless series of variations on this major theme, namely, that "democracy is under attack" by a conspiracy of Russians and neo-Nazis that magically materialized out of the ether during the Summer of 2016. The intelligence agencies, political elites, academia, celebrities, social media personalities, and other organs of the culture industry have been systematically reifying this official narrative through constant repetition. The Western masses have been inundated with innumerable articles, editorials, television news and talk show segments, books, social media posts, and various other forms of messaging whipping up hysteria over "Russians" and "fascists."

At this point, it is no longer just propaganda. It has become the new "Truth." It has become "reality."

Becoming "reality" is, of course, the ultimate goal of every ideology. An ideology is just a system of ideas, and is thus fair game for critique and dissent. Reality is not fair game for dissent. It is not up for debate or challenge, not by "serious," "legitimate" people. Reality is simply "the way it is." It is axiomatic. It is apothegmatic. It's not a belief or an interpretation. It is not subject to change or revision. It is the immortal, immutable Word of God, or whatever deity or deity-like concept the ruling classes and the masses they rule accept

---

1 *Hopkins, C. J., "The War on Dissent," Consent Factory, January 26, 2018*

as the Final Arbiter of Truth. In our case, this would be Science, or Reason, rather than some supernatural being, but in terms of ideology there isn't much difference. Every system of belief, regardless of its nature, ultimately depends on political power and power relations to enforce its beliefs, which is to say, to make them "real."

OK, whenever I write about "reality" and "truth," I get a few rather angry responses from folks who appear to think I'm denying the existence of objective reality. I'm not ... for example, this chair I'm sitting on is absolutely part of objective reality, a physical object that actually exists. The page or screen you are reading these words on is also part of objective reality.

I am not saying there is no reality.

What I'm saying is, "reality" is a concept, a concept invented and developed by people. A concept that serves a variety of purposes, some philosophical, some political.

It's the political purposes I am interested in.

Think of "reality" as an ideological tool. A tool in the hands of those with the power to designate what is "real" and what isn't. Doctors, teachers, politicians, police, scientists, priests, pundits, experts, parents — these are the enforcers of "reality."

The powerless do not get to decide what is "real." Ask someone suffering from schizophrenia. Or ... I'm sorry, is it bipolar disorder? Or oppositional defiant disorder? I can't keep all these new disorders psychiatrists keep "discovering" straight.

Or ask a Palestinian living in Gaza. Or the mother of a Black kid the cops shot for no reason. Ask Julian Assange. Or the families of all those "enemy combatants" Obama droned.

Ask the "conspiracy theorists" on Twitter digitally screaming at anyone who will listen about what is and isn't "the truth."

Each of them will give you their version of reality, and you and I might agree with some of them, and some of their beliefs may be supported with facts, but that will not make what they believe reality.

Power is what makes "reality" reality.

Not facts.

Not evidence.

Not knowledge.

Power.

Those in power, or aligned with those in power, or parroting the narratives of those in power, understand this (whether consciously or not). Those without power mostly do not, and thus we continue to "speak truth to power," as if those in power gave a shit.

They don't. The powerful are not arguing with us. They are not attempting to win a debate about what is and isn't true, or what did or didn't "really" happen. They are declaring what did or didn't happen. They are telling us what is and is not "reality," and demonstrating what happens to those who disagree.

The "Democracy versus The Putin-Nazis" narrative is our new "reality," whether we like it or not. It does not matter one iota that there is zero evidence to support this narrative, other than the claims of Intelligence agencies, politicians, the corporate media, and other servants of the ruling classes.

The Russians are "attacking democracy" because the ruling classes tell us they are. "Fascism is on the march again" because the ruling classes say it is. Anyone who disagrees is a "Putin-sympathizer," a "Putin-apologist," or "linked to Russia," or "favored by Russia," or an "anti-Semite," or a "fascist apologist."

Question the official narrative about the Gratuitously Baby Gassing Monster of Syria and you're an "Assad apologist," a "Russian bot network," or a "plagiarizing Red-Brown infiltrator." Criticize the corporate media for disseminating cheap McCarthyite smears, and you are a Tulsi-stanning, Hindu Nazi-apologist.[2] God help you if you should appear on FOX, in which case you are a Nazi-legitimizer![3] A cursory check of the Internet today revealed that "far-right Facebook groups are spreading hate to millions in Europe"[4] by means of some hypnogenic content that just looking at it turns you into a Nazi. Our democracy-loving friends at The Atlantic Council are disappointed

---

2 Taibbi, Matt, "We've Hit a New Low in Campaign Hit Pieces," Rolling Stone, May 21, 2019 ("Last week, the Daily Beast ran this headline: 'Tulsi Gabbard's Campaign Is Being Boosted by Putin Apologists.' That was followed by the sub headline: 'The Hawaii congresswoman is quickly becoming the top candidate for Democrats who think the Russian leader is misunderstood.' The Gabbard campaign has received 75,000 individual donations. This crazy Beast article is based on (maybe) three of them.")

3 CounterPunch editor Joshua Frank on Twitter, May 14, 2019 ("Naw, when you go on Fox you legitimize their right-wing propaganda.")

4 Graham-Harrison, Emma, "Far-right Facebook groups 'spreading hate to millions in Europe'," The Guardian, May 22, 2019

by Trump's refusal to sign the so-called "Christchurch Call," a multilateral statement encouraging corporations to censor the Internet[5] ... and fascism is fashionable in Italy again!"[6]

This post-Orwellian, neo-McCarthyite mass hysteria is not going to stop, not until the global capitalist ruling classes have suppressed the current "populist" insurgency and restored "normality" throughout the Western world.[7] Until then, it's going to be pretty much non-stop "Democracy versus the Putin-Nazis."

So, unless you're enjoying our new reality, or are willing to conform to it for some other reason, prepare to be smeared as "a Russia-loving, Putin-apologizing conspiracy theorist," or a "fascism-enabling, Trump-loving Nazi," or some other type of insidiously Slavic, white supremacist, mass-murder enthusiast.

Things are only going to get uglier as the American election season ramps up. I mean, come on ... you don't really believe that the global capitalist ruling classes are going to let Trump serve a second term, do you?

---

5 Brooking, Emerson T., "The Christchurch call and the failure of US leadership," Atlantic Council, New Atlanticist, May 20, 2019

6 David, Ariel, "Black Is Back: How Fascism Is Fashionable in Italy (Again)," Haaretz, May 14, 2019

7 Klein, Ezra, "Joe Biden's promise: a return to normalcy," Vox, May 20, 2019

The Hitlerization of Jeremy Corbyn

June 13, 2019

Every time you think the corporatocracy's manufactured anti-Semitism hysteria cannot possibly get any more absurd, they somehow manage to outdo themselves.

OK, stay with me now, because this is a weird one.

Apparently, American Hitler and his cronies are conspiring with a group of "Jewish leaders" to stop British Hitler from becoming prime minister and wiping out all the Jews in Great Britain. Weird, right? But that's not the weird part, because maybe American Hitler wants to wipe out all the Jews in Great Britain himself, rather than leaving it to British Hitler (Hitlers being notoriously jealous regarding their genocidal accomplishments).

No, the weird part is that everyone knows that American Hitler does not make a move without the approval of Russian Hitler, who is also obsessed with wiping out the Jews, and with destroying the fabric of Western democracy. So why would Russian Hitler want to let American Hitler and his goons thwart the ascendancy of British Hitler, who, in addition to wanting to wipe out all the Jews, also wants to destroy democracy by fascistically refunding the NHS, re-nationalizing the British rail system, and so on?

It doesn't make a whole lot of sense, does it? In any event, here's the official story.

In "a recording leaked to *The Washington Post*,"[1] and then flogged by the rest of the corporate media, Reichsminister des Auswärtigen, Mike Pompeo, told a group of unnamed "Jewish leaders" that American Hitler (i.e., Donald Trump) will "push back" (i.e., intervene) against British Hitler (i.e., Jeremy Corbyn) to protect the lives of Jews in Great Britain if British Hitler becomes prime min-

1 Mason, Rowena and Stewart, Heather, "Mike Pompeo tells Jewish leaders he would 'push back' against Corbyn," The Guardian, June 9, 2019

ister (and is possibly already doing so now). The identities of these "Jewish leaders" have not been disclosed by the corporate media, presumably in order to protect them from being murdered by Corbyn's Nazi hit squad. Whoever they were, they wanted to know whether American Hitler and his fascist cabinet were "willing to work with [them] to take on actions if life becomes very difficult for Jews" after Jeremy Corbyn seizes power, declares himself Führer of Communist Britannia, and orders the immediate invasion of France.

To anyone who has been closely following the corporate media's relentless coverage of Jeremy Corbyn's Nazi Death Cult (i.e., the UK Labour Party) and the global Anti-Semitism Pandemic, it comes as no real surprise that this group of "Jewish leaders" (whoever they are) would want to stop him from becoming prime minister. I doubt that their motives have much to do with fighting anti-Semitism, or anything else specifically "Jewish," but ... well, I'm kind of old-fashioned that way. I still believe that there's a fundamental difference between "the Jews" and the global capitalist ruling classes.

I realize that both the neoliberal establishment and the neo-fascist fringe disagree with me, and that both are determined (for different reasons) to conflate the two in the public's mind, but that's my take, and I'm sticking to it.

I don't think the world is controlled by "the Jews." I think it's controlled by global capitalism.

Go ahead, call me a conspiracy theorist.

Here's how the anti-Semitism panic in the United Kingdom looks to me.

After nearly forty years of privatization and restructuring, British society is on the brink of being permanently transformed into the type of savage, neo-feudal, corporatist nightmare that the USA already is. The global capitalist ruling classes are extremely pleased about this state of affairs. They would now like to finish up privatizing Britain, so they can get on with privatizing the rest of Europe. The last thing they need at this critical juncture is Jeremy Corbyn to become prime minister and start attempting to remake their nascent neoliberal marketplace into a society ... you know, where healthcare is guaranteed to all, you don't need a mortgage to buy a train ticket, and people don't have to eat out of trash bins.

Unlike in the USA, where there is no functional political Left, and where the non-parliamentary "two-party system" is almost totally controlled by the corporatocracy, in the UK, there are still a few old-fashioned socialists, and they have taken back the Labour Party from the neoliberal Blairite stooges that had been managing the transformation of Britain into the aforementioned neo-feudal nightmare. Jeremy Corbyn is the leader of these socialists. So the corporatocracy needs to destroy him, take back control of the Labour Party, and turn it back into a fake left party, like the Democratic Party in the USA, so they can concentrate on crushing the right-wing populists. Thus, they need to Hitlerize Corbyn, so they can fold him into their official narrative, Democracy vs. The Putin-Nazis.

And, see, this is what makes the corporatocracy's War on Populism so seemingly psychotic ... at least to anyone paying attention.

In the USA, the populist insurgency is primarily a right-wing phenomenon (because, again, there is no Left to speak of). Thus, the neoliberal ruling classes are focused on Hitlerizing Donald Trump, and stigmatizing the millions of Americans who voted for him as a bunch of "Nazis." Hitlerizing Trump has been ridiculously easy (he almost Hitlerizes himself), but the ultimate goal is to delegitimize the populist sentiment that put him into office. That sentiment is primarily neo-nationalist. So it's a one-front counter-insurgency op (i.e., neoliberalism versus neo-nationalism).

In the UK, things are not that simple. There, the neoliberal ruling classes are waging a counter-insurgency op against populist forces on two major fronts: (1) the Brexiters (i.e., nationalism); and (2) the Corbynists (i.e., socialism). They're getting hit from both the left and right, which is screwing up the official narrative (according to which the "enemies of democracy" are supposed to be right-wing neo-nationalists). So, as contradictory and absurd as it sounds, they needed to conflate both left and right populism into one big scary Hitlerian enemy. Thus, they needed to Hitlerize Corbyn.

Presto ... Labour Anti-Semitism crisis!

Now, anyone who is isn't a gibbering idiot knows that Jeremy Corbyn is not an anti-Semite and the Labour Party is not a hive of Nazis. It's a testament to the power of the corporate media that such a statement even needs to be made ... but, of course, that's the point of the smear campaign the neoliberal corporate media have been waging for the last three years.

Smear campaigns are simple and effective. The goal is to force your target and his allies into proclaiming things like, "I am not an anti-Semite," or "I've never had sex with underage boys," or whatever smear you want to force them to deny. You don't have to prove your target guilty. You're just trying to conjure up a "reality" in which every time anyone thinks of your target they associate him with the content of your smears.

The corporate media have done just that, to Jeremy Corbyn, to Donald Trump, to Putin, and to assorted lesser figures. They did it to Sanders in 2016.[2] They are doing it now to Tulsi Gabbard.[3] The goal is not only to smear these targets, but also, and more so, to conjure a "world" that reifies the narrative of their smears … a binary "good versus evil" world, a world in which whatever they want to accuse their targets of being linked to (e.g., terrorism, fascism, racism, or whatever) is the official enemy of all that is good.

Since the Brexit referendum and the election of Trump, the ruling classes have conjured up a world where "democracy" is perpetually under attack by a global conspiracy of "Russians" and "Nazis" (just as they previously conjured up a world where it was perpetually under attack by "terrorists"). They have conjured up a post-Orwellian reality in which "democracy" (i.e., global capitalism) is the only alternative to "neo-fascism" (i.e., anything opposed to global capitalism).

And this is why Corbyn had to be Hitlerized, and why Putin, Trump, Assad, Gabbard, Assange, the "Yellow Vest" protesters in France, and anyone else opposing global neoliberalism has to be Hitlerized. Socialism, nationalism … it makes no difference, not to the global capitalist ruling classes. There are always only two sides in these "worlds" that the ruling classes conjure up for us, and there can be only one official enemy. The official enemy of the moment is "fascism." Therefore, all the "bad guys" are Hitler, or Nazis, or racists, or anti-Semites, or some other variation of Hitler.

---

2 Sanders, Sam, "Bernie Sanders Faces Criticism Over Comments On Race," National Public Radio, March 7, 2016

3 Tani, Maxwell and Weill, Kelly, "Why Conservative Media and the Far Right Love Tulsi Gabbard for President," Daily Beast, January 15, 2019

The fact that this "reality" they have conjured up for us is completely psychotic makes it no less real. And it is only going to get more insane until the corporatocracy restores "normality." So, go ahead, if you consider yourself "normal," and try to force your mind to believe that Jews are no longer safe in Great Britain, or in Germany, or France, or the USA, and that Donald Trump is a Russian asset, and is also literally Adolf Hitler, and an anti-Semitic white supremacist who is conspiring with Israel and Saudi Arabia in their campaign to destroy Iran and Syria, which are allies of his Russian masters, as is Venezuela, which he is also menacing, and that Jeremy Corbyn's secret plan is to turn the UK into Nazi Germany, with the support of Trump, who is trying to destroy him, and that the Yellow Vests are Russian-backed fascists, and that Julian Assange is a rapist spy who conspired with Russia to get Trump elected, which is why Trump wants to prosecute him, just as soon as he finishes wiping out the Jews, or protecting them from Jeremy Corbyn, or from Iran, or brainwashing Black Americans into reelecting him in 2020 with a handful of Russian Facebook ads.

Go ahead, try to reconcile all that … or whatever, don't. Just take whatever medication you happen to be on, crank up CNN, MSNBC, or any other corporate media channel, and report me to the Internet Police for posting dangerous "extremist" content.

You know, in your heart, I probably deserve it.

The United States of Fascism Hysteria

July 10, 2019

So, it has been an exciting few weeks for Antifa and the rest of the neoliberal Resistance. OK, they haven't yet managed to overthrow the Putin-Nazi occupation government (hereinafter "POG"), but they have definitely got "the Fash" on the run.

Fascism hysteria is spreading like wildfire. Liberal Twitter mobs are out for blood. At this point, it's only a matter of time until the sleeping giant of normality awakens and purges America of the fascist filth that have Putin-Nazified this once great nation.

Antifa has been at the vanguard of the fight, smashing the Fash on both East and West Coasts. In Portland, where a gang of neo-fascist anti-masturbationists known as the "Proud Boys" had assembled for a self-promotional street fight they were billing as the "Battle of Portland 2," Antifa militants positively identified and preventatively beat the living snot out of a journalist named Andy Ngo.[1] To prevent him from snitching to the fascist cops (who are allegedly working hand in hand with the POG), they self-defensively robbed him, sprayed him with silly string, and pelted him with vegan milkshakes.

Now, before you get all up in arms about Antifa assaulting and robbing journalists, you need to know a couple things. First, according to Antifa spokespersons, and those bloodthirsty liberal Twitter mobs, Andy Ngo is a "fascist adjacent," and possibly even a card carrying fascist.

Antifa representative Alexander Reid Ross (who, in addition to lecturing at some college in Oregon, is renowned for his work on the neo-Strasserist-Duginist-Putin-Nazi conspiracy to infiltrate the Left and take over the whole world)[2] claims that Ngo is personally

---

1 Editorial Board, "Antifa Attacks a Journalist," The Wall Street Journal, July 1, 2019

2 Ross, Alexander Reid, "Fascism and the Far Left: A Grim Global Love Affair," Haaretz, May 27, 2019

responsible for putting people's names on a Nazi "kill-list," or at least that Ngo's writing has been published by *Quillette*, which published an article by someone else that some fascists read and copied people's names from,[3] so, basically, he deserves to die.

Also, assaulting and robbing Ngo was technically "preemptive self-defense"[4] (you know, like when we invaded Iraq to defend ourselves from those WMDs). Despite their helmets and body armor, and the fact that Ngo is a doughy little gay guy, his presence among them on a public street was making Antifa feel "unsafe." So, they had no choice but to beat him senseless, steal his camera, and vegan milkshake him.

As Antifa expert Mark Bray explains, when you're Antifa, "fighting back is always self-defense, even if [you] strike the first blow."[5] (This logic only applies to anti-fascists, of course, like Antifa and the US military, and not to, you know, gangs of thugs, or the perpetrators of wars of aggression.)

Antifa's self-defensive mugging of a journalist apparently scared the crap out of POG, because one week later, back in Washington, DC, President Hitler called in the tanks, and the Luftwaffe, and announced that he was going to stage a reenactment of a Nuremberg Rally right in front of the Lincoln Memorial.

The liberal intelligentsia went apeshit. This was really it this time! Putin had given Trump the green-light to declare martial law and pronounce himself Führer. The long-awaited Putin-Nazi Apocalypse was finally about to begin!

Unfortunately, Trump's Fourth of July Jamboree turned out to be a rather tame affair. He even almost made it through his speech without making an ass of himself.[6] This was extremely disappointing for liberals, who were hoping he would go full-Hitler, paint "death's

---

3 Alexander Reid-Ross on Twitter, June 30, 2019 ("I was put on an Atomwaffen kill list of journalists taken straight from an article published at Quillette where he's an editor. Last year, I was punched in the face by a Proud Boy on film while reporting, but Andy was too busy playing victim to mind. His 'work' supports violence.")

4 Vysotsky, Stanislav, "Antifa in America: Militant Anti-fascism Isn't Terrorism, It's Self-defense," Haaretz, July 3, 2019

5 Karlin, Mark, "'At Its Core, Anti-Fascism Is Self-Defense': An Interview With Mark Bray," Truthout, February 11, 2018

6 Liptak, Kevin, "Trump blames faulty teleprompter for snafu about 'airports' during the Revolutionary War," CNN, July 5, 2019

heads" on the turrets of the Bradleys, and a swastika on the tail of Air Force One, and order ICE to start rounding up the Jews.

The weekend wasn't a total let-down, however. The Proud Boys (who are obviously gluttons for punishment), staged yet another self-promotional event, this one billed as "Defend Free Speech." A few hundred people turned up to listen to speeches by a handful of Alt-Right clowns desperately trying to reignite their careers. They were outnumbered 2-to-1 by Antifa, Black Lives Matter, assorted drag queens, and an indigenous, two-spirited transperson of color, who reportedly "performed a spoken word" on the meaning of the term "Latinx."

The DC police (who are even more "fascist" than the Portland police who stood by and watched as Antifa beat up and robbed a journalist) fascistically prevented Antifa militants from storming into the Alt-Right rally and beating the snot out of everyone in sight. So, the anti-fascists had no choice but to preemptively attack a newspaper dispenser, which was presumably making them feel "unsafe," or disseminating POG propaganda, or something. One of them tried to burn a flag, but he couldn't figure out how to operate his matches. Assorted other hilarious acts of revolutionary direct action followed. Apparently, Antifa's strategy was to smash the Fash by amusing them to death.

Meanwhile, militant Resistance actions against the infamous POG "concentration camps" continue. New York City, San Francisco, and other liberal metropolitan areas have almost completely emptied out as liberals flock to the southern border to liberate the surviving prisoners. Conditions in the camps are now beyond inhuman. According to Alexandria Ocasio-Cortez, migrants are being forced to drink out of toilets,[7] and otherwise subjected to "systematic cruelty"[8] (so you can understand why liberals are physically putting their bodies on the line to bring an end to this horrifying sadism, and not just sitting around on the Internet shrieking about "concentration

---

7 Rennix, Brianna and Robinson, Nathan, "Crammed into cells and forced to drink from the toilet – this is how the US treats migrants," The Guardian, July 3, 2019 (The "toilets" in question were the standard metal all-in-one units featured in most prisons and detention centers, in which the toilet is below and the sink is above.)

8 Montoya-Galvez, Camilo, "Alexandria Ocasio-Cortez decries 'systemic cruelty' after visiting migrant detention center," CBS News, July 1, 2019

camps" as they travel to their summer holiday rentals on Martha's Vineyard, or the Hamptons, or wherever).

No, these Putin-Nazi "concentration camps" are nothing at all like the "detention facilities" the Obama administration operated, even though they look exactly the same.[9] Sure, thousands of migrant children were separated from their parents, in cages, and there were tens of thousands of incidents of rape, sexual abuse, and beatings,[10] and so on, but, otherwise, these Obama "detention facilities" were more like great big 2-star hotels, or like student dorms at a state university, so there was no need for liberals to get all worked up and start comparing them to places like Dachau and Buchenwald.

Plus, the media published a heartbreaking picture of a dead little girl![11] So just shut up about Obama already! Enough with history, critical thinking, and the practical aspects of immigration policy! It's time to abolish all national borders, issue everyone a US passport, and transcend the whole concept of national sovereignty, or at least to provide the capitalist ruling classes with an endless supply of cheap, undocumented, extremely compliant unskilled labor.

Those Bel Air lawns aren't going to mow themselves!

Jesus, I can't believe I just wrote that. Concentration camps and dead people are nothing to joke about. It's OK, however, to cynically use them to whip people up into a paroxysm of manufactured mass fascism hysteria. Not that the neoliberal ruling classes and the corporate media would ever do that. No, they would never repeatedly attempt to evoke our hatred of the actual Nazis (and their actual concentration camps, which people were dragged out of their homes, loaded onto trains, and shipped away to, and which you could not voluntarily depart) in order to short-circuit our critical thinking, or otherwise emotionally manipulate us into supporting their War on Populism.

---

9 Johnson, Benny, "Here Are The Photos Of Obama's Illegal Immigrant Detention Facilities The Media Won't Show You," Daily Caller, June 19, 2019 (The photos are indistinguishable from the detention facilities used by the Trump administration.)

10 "A Culture of Cruelty," a 2011 report by No More Deaths (nomoredeaths.org), documenting approximately 30,000 cases of rape, sexual abuse, beating and other abuses prepetrated against child and adult migrants during the early Obama years.

11 Hartley-Parkinson, Richard, "Devastating picture of dead migrant girl and her dad trying to get to the US," Metro, June 26, 2019 (This was the widely-disseminated AFP photo of the dead little girl and her father lying face down on the riverbank.)

No, the "Putin-Nazi occupation government" is not just manufactured mass hysteria concocted by the neoliberal ruling classes. Donald Trump is literally a Nazi. There's a portrait of Hitler in the Oval Office. Putin really controls America. Putin, and his cabal of Russian Nazis. They're everywhere. They own the banks. They control the media. They control elections. They are the "International Invisible Government." (Is any of this sounding vaguely familiar?) They are devising the Final Solution to the Immigrant Problem right this minute. They are doing this at Mar-a-Lago, where Trump has had a big "Black Sun" etched into the marble floor.

So, if you're serious about your anti-fascism, now's the time to load up on silly string, ski goggles, masks, hard knuckle gloves, and whatever you make those milkshakes with. POG might be on the run at the moment, but there's an election season coming up, so we need to be prepared for anything.

The important thing is to remain hysterical, and to be ready to respond to whatever emotional stimuli the ruling classes wave in our faces. The fate of democracy hangs in the balance.

Oh, and watch out for those fascist newspaper dispensers!

The War on White-Supremacist Terror

August 8, 2019

If you enjoyed the global corporatocracy's original War on Islamicist Terror, you're going to love their latest spinoff … The War on White-Supremacist Terror. It's basically just like the old War on Terror, except that this time the bad guys are all white supremacists, and Donald Trump is Osama bin Laden … unless Putin is Osama bin Laden. OK, I'm not quite sure who's Osama bin Laden. Whatever. The point is, the Terrorists are coming!

Yes, that's right, some racist psycho murdered a bunch of people in Texas, so it's time to "take the gloves off" again, pass some new kind of Patriot Act, further curtail our civil liberties, and generally whip the public up into a mass hysteria over "white supremacist terrorism."

The New York Times Editorial Board is already hard at work on that front. In a lengthy op-ed that ran last Sunday, "We Have a White Nationalist Terrorist Problem,"[1] the Board proposes that we would all be safer if the government — but presumably not the current government — could arbitrarily deem people "terrorists," or "potential terrorists," or "terrorist sympathizers," regardless of whether they have any connection to any actual terrorist groups, and … well, here's what the Editorial Board has in mind.

> "The resources of the American government and its international allies would mobilize without delay. The awesome power of the state would work tirelessly to deny future terrorists access to weaponry, money and forums to spread their ideology. The movement would be infiltrated by spies and informants. Its financiers would face sanctions. Places of congregation would be surveilled. Those who gave aid or comfort to terrorists would be prosecuted."

1 *The Editorial Board, "We Have a White Nationalist Terrorist Problem," The New York Times, August 5, 2019*

The Board didn't mention the offshore gulags, wars of aggression, assassinations, torture, mass surveillance of virtually everyone, and other such features of the original War on Terror, but presumably all that kind of stuff would be included in "the awesome power of the state" that the Board would like the US government to "mobilize without delay."

And the mandarins of *The New York Times* were just getting started with the terrorism hysteria. The Tuesday edition was brimming with references to "white supremacy" and "domestic terrorism." Here are some of the front page headlines. "Trump is a White Supremacist Who Inspires Terrorism."[2] "White Terrorism Shows Parallels to Islamic State."[3] "The Nihilist in Chief: how our president and our mass shooters are connected to the same dark psychic forces."[4] "I Spent 25 Years Fighting Jihadis. White Supremacists Aren't So Different."[5] "Trump, Tax Cuts, and Terrorism."[6] And so on.

The *Times* was hardly alone, of course. In the wake of the El Paso and Dayton shootings, the corporate media went into overdrive, pumping out "white supremacist terrorism" mass hysteria around the clock. *The Guardian* took a break from smearing Jeremy Corbyn as an anti-Semite to proclaim that El Paso was "Trump-inspired Terrorism."[7] *The Sydney Morning Herald* declared that the US is now officially in the throes of a "white nationalist terrorism crisis."[8] *The Atlantic* likened Trump to Anwar al-Awlaki,[9] and assured us that "the worst is yet to come!"[10] Liberal journalists and politicians rushed

---

2 Goldberg, Michelle, "Trump Is a White Nationalist Who Inspires Terrorism," The New York Times, August 5, 2019

3 Fisher, Max, "White Terrorism Shows 'Stunning' Parallels to Islamic State's Rise," The New York Times, August 6, 2019

4 Douthat, Ross, "The Nihilist in Chief," The New York Times, August 6, 2019

5 Soufan, Ali H., "I Spent 25 Years Fighting Jihadis. White Supremacists Aren't So Different," The New York Times, August 5, 2019

6 Krugman, Paul, "Trump, Tax Cuts and Terrorism," The New York Times, August 5, 2019

7 Schanzer, David, "We must call the El Paso shooting what it is: Trump-inspired terrorism," The Guardian, August 5, 2019

8 Werlman, C. J., "US in the midst of a white nationalist terrorism crisis," The Sydney Morning Herald, August 4, 2019

9 McQuade, Barbara, "A Charismatic Leader for White Nationalists," The Atlantic, August 6, 2019

10 Bayoumy, Yara and Gilsinan, Kathy, "A Reformed White Nationalist Says the Worst Is Yet to Come," The Atlantic, August 6, 2019

onto Twitter to inform their followers that a global conspiracy of white supremacist terrorists "emboldened" or "inspired" by Donald Trump (who, remember, is a Russian secret agent) is threatening the very fabric of democracy, so it's time to take some extraordinary measures!

Never mind that it turns out that two of the three "white supremacist terrorist" mass murderers in question (i.e., the Gilroy, El Paso, and Dayton shooters) do not appear to have been white supremacists or that none of them were linked to any terrorist groups. We're living in the Age of Non-Terrorist Terrorism,[11] in which anyone can be deemed a "terrorist," or a "suddenly self-radicalized terrorist," regardless of whether they have any actual connection to organized terrorism.

Terrorism isn't what used to be. Back in the day (i.e, the 1970s), there were terrorist groups like the PFLP, ANO, BSO, IRA, RAF, FARC, the Weather Underground, and so on … in other words, actual terrorist groups, committing acts of actual terrorism. More recently, there was al Qaeda and ISIS. Nowadays, however, more or less any attention-seeking sociopath with a death wish and a knock-off AR-15 (or moron with a bunch of non-exploding pipe bombs)[12] can be deemed a bona fide "domestic terrorist," as long as it serves the global capitalist ruling classes' official narrative.

The official narrative of the moment is Democracy versus The Putin-Nazis (also known as The War on Populism), which I've been covering in these columns, satirically and more seriously, for the better part of the last three years.

According to this official narrative, "democracy is under attack" by a conspiracy of Russians and neo-Nazis that magically materialized out of thin air during the Summer of 2016, right around the time Trump won the nomination. OK, the Russia part kind of sputtered out recently, so the global capitalist ruling classes and their mouthpieces in the corporate media are now going full-bore on the fascism hysteria. They've been doing this relentlessly since Trump won the

---

11 Hopkins, C. J., "The Dawning of the Age of Non-Terrorist Terrorism," CounterPunch, August 1, 2016

12 Scutti, Susan, "Cesar Sayoc, who sent pipe bombs to prominent Democrats, sentenced to 20 years," CNN, August 6, 2019

election, alternating between the Russia hysteria and the fascism hysteria from week to week, day to day, sometimes hour to hour, depending on which one is "hot" at the moment.

These recent mass shootings have provided the capitalist ruling classes with a golden opportunity, not just to flog the fascism hysteria once again, but to fold it into the terrorism hysteria which Americans have been indoctrinated with since September 11, 2001 (the objective of which indoctrination being to establish in the American psyche "the Terrorist" as the new official enemy, replacing the "Communist" official enemy that had filled this role throughout the Cold War). If you think the original War on Terror was just about oil or geopolitical hegemony, check out "leftist" political Twitter's response to the El Paso and Dayton shootings. You'll find, not just hysterical liberals, but "leftists" and even so-called "anarchists," shrieking about "white supremacist terrorism." It was the number one Twitter hashtag on Monday.

No, the original War on Terror (whatever else it was) was probably the most effective fascist psy-op in the history of fascist psy-ops. Fifteen years of relentless exposure to manufactured "terrorism" hysteria has conditioned most Americans (and most Westerners, generally), upon hearing emotional trigger words like "terrorist" and "terrorism" emanating from the mouths of politicians (or the front page of *The New York Times*) to immediately switch off their critical thinking, and start demanding that the authorities censor the Internet, suspend the US Constitution, and fill the streets with militarized vehicles and special "anti-terror" forces with assault rifles in the "sling-ready" position. This tweet by Geraldo Rivera captures the authoritarian mindset perfectly:

> "In the meantime, there must be active-shooter trained, heavily armed security personnel every place innocents are gathered."[13]

I'm not quite sure what "in the meantime" means. Perhaps it means until the USA, Western Europe, and the rest of the empire, can be transformed into a happy, hate-free, supranational corporate police state where there is no racism, no fascism, no terrorism, and no one ever says bad things on the Internet.

13 Geraldo Rivera on Twitter, August 4, 2019

What a glorious, transhuman world that will be, like a living, breathing Benetton ad, once all the racists, terrorists, and extremists have been eliminated, or heavily medicated, or quarantined and reeducated!

Until then, the War on White Supremacist Terrorism, Domestic Terrorism, Islamic Terrorism, Russian Terrorism, Iranian Terrorism, anti-Semitic Labour Party Terrorism, and any other type of terrorism, extremism, hate, conspiratorial thinking ... oh, and Populism (I almost forgot that one), and every other type of non-conformity to global capitalist ideology, will continue until we achieve final victory!

It's coming ... sooner than you probably think.

Damn, here I am, at the end of my essay, and I almost forget to call Trump a racist. He is, of course. He's a big fat racist. I should have put that right at the top. I'm already in hot water with my fellow leftists for not doing that enough. Oh, and for the record, in case there are any other kinds of Inquisitors reading this, I also renounce Satan and all his works.

The Future of the Spectacle, or: How the West Learned to Stop Worrying and Love the Reality Police

September 3, 2019

If you want a vision of the future, don't imagine "a boot stamping on a human face — for ever," as Orwell suggested in *1984*. Instead, imagine that human face staring mesmerized into the screen of some of nifty, futuristic device on which every word, sound, and image has been algorithmically approved for consumption by the Defense Advanced Research Projects Agency ("DARPA") and its "innovation ecosystem" of "academic, corporate, and governmental partners."

The screen of this futuristic device will offer a virtually unlimited range of "non-divisive" and "hate-free" content, none of which will falsify or distort the "truth," or in any way deviate from "reality."

Western consumers will finally be free to enjoy an assortment of news, opinion, entertainment, and educational content (like the recent *Guardian* podcast about "a man who gave birth,"[1] or MSNBC's latest bombshell about Donald Trump's secret Russian oligarch backers)[2] without having their enjoyment totally ruined by discord-sowing alternative journalists like Aaron Maté or satirists like myself.

---

1 "The man who gave birth," The Guardian, September 2, 2019 (A podcast presented by Anushka Asthana with Freddy McConnell and Andrew Rawnsley)

2 "MSNBC's Lawrence O'Donnell hits Russiagate rock bottom," The Grayzone, August 31, 2019 ("Aaron Maté slams MSNBC's latest Russiagate dud, exposing how Lawrence O'Donnell's embarrassing retraction is part of a pattern of bogus conspiracy theories.")

"Fake news" will not appear on this screen. All the news will be "authentic." DARPA and its partners will see to that. You won't have to worry about being "influenced" by Russians, Nazis, conspiracy theorists, socialists, populists, extremists, or whomever. Such Persons of Malicious Intent will still be able to post their content (because of "freedom of speech" and all that stuff), but they will do so down in the sewers of the Internet where normal consumers won't have to see it. Anyone who ventures down there looking for it (i.e., such "divisive" and "polarizing" content) will be immediately placed on an official DARPA watchlist for "potential extremists," or "potential white supremacists," or "potential Russians."

Once that happens, their lives will be over (i.e., the lives of the potentially extremist fools who have logged onto whatever dark web platform will still be posting essays like this, not the lives of the Persons of Malicious Intent, who never had any lives to begin with, and who by that time will probably be operating out of some heavily armed, off-the-grid compound in Idaho). Their schools, employers, and landlords will be notified. Their photos and addresses will be published online. Anyone who ever said two words to them (or, God help them, appears in a photograph with them) will have 24 hours to publicly denounce them, or be placed on DARPA's watchlist themselves.

Meanwhile, up where the air is clean, Western consumers will sit in their cubicles, or stagger blindly down the sidewalk like zombies, or come barrel-assing at you on their pink corporate scooters, staring down at the screens of their devices, where normal reality will be unfolding. They will stare at their screens at their dinner tables, in restaurants, in bed, and everywhere else. Every waking hour of their lives will be spent consuming the all-consuming, smiley, happy, global-capitalist Spectacle, every empty moment of which will be monitored and pre-approved by DARPA.

What a relief that will finally be, not to have to question anything, or wonder what is real and what isn't! When the media tell us the Russians hacked an election, or the Vermont power grid,[3]

3 Eilperin, Juliet and Entous, Adam, "Russian operation hacked a Vermont utility, showing risk to U.S. electrical grid security, officials say," The Washington Post, December 30, 2016

or are blackmailing the president with an FSB pee-tape,[4] or that the non-corporate media are all "propaganda peddlers,"[5] or that the Labour Party is a hive of anti-Semites,[6] or that some bogeyman has WMDs,[7] or is yanking little babies out of their incubators,[8] or gratuitously gassing them,[9] or attacking us with crickets,[10] or that someone secretly met with Julian Assange in the Ecuadorian embassy,[11] or that we're being attacked by Russian spy whales,[12] and suddenly self-radicalized Nazi terrorists,[13] or that it's time for the "International Community" to humanitarianly intervene[14] because

4 Chait, Jonathan, "The Steele Dossier on Trump and Russia Is Looking More and More Real," New York Magazine, December 7, 2017

5 Timberg, Craig, "Russian propaganda effort helped spread fake news during election, experts say," The Washington Post, November 24, 2016

6 See, e.g., FiveFilters' list of over one hundred Guardian articles spreading spurious charges of the Labour Party's "antisemitism." (https://theguardian.fivefilters.org/antisemitism/)

7 Borger, Julian, "There were no weapons of mass destruction in Iraq," The Guardian, October 7, 2004

8 Stauber, John and Rampton, Sheldon, Toxic Sludge is Good for You, Common Courage Press, 1995 ("In fact, the most emotionally moving testimony on October 10 came from a 15-year-old Kuwaiti girl, known only by her first name of Nayirah ... Sobbing, she described what she had seen with her own eyes in a hospital in Kuwait City. Her written testimony was passed out in a media kit prepared by Citizens for a Free Kuwait. "I volunteered at the al-Addan hospital," Nayirah said. "While I was there, I saw the Iraqi soldiers come into the hospital with guns, and go into the room where ... babies were in incubators. They took the babies out of the incubators, took the incubators, and left the babies on the cold floor to die." At the Human Rights Caucus, however, Hill & Knowlton and Congressman Lantos had failed to reveal that Nayirah was a member of the Kuwaiti Royal Family. Her father, in fact, was Saud Nasir al-Sabah, Kuwait's Ambassador to the US, who sat listening in the hearing room during her testimony. The Caucus also failed to reveal that H&K vice-president Lauri Fitz-Pegado had coached Nayirah in what even the Kuwaitis' own investigators later confirmed was false testimony.")

9 Fisk, Robert, "The evidence we were never meant to see about the Douma 'gas' attack," The Independent, May 23, 2019 ("[I]n the last few days, there has emerged disturbing evidence that in its final report on the alleged use of chemical weapons by the Syrian regime in the city of Douma last year, the OPCW deliberately concealed from both the public and the press the existence of a dissenting 15-page assessment of two cylinders which had supposedly contained molecular chlorine – perhaps the most damning evidence against the Assad regime in the entire report.")

10 Zimmer, Carl, "The Sounds That Haunted U.S. Diplomats in Cuba? Lovelorn Crickets, Scientists Say," The New York Times, January 4, 2019

11 Greenwald, Glenn, "Five Weeks After The Guardian's Viral Blockbuster Assange-Manafort Scoop, No Evidence Has Emerged — Just Stonewalling," The Intercept, January 2, 2019

12 Ellis-Peterson, Hannah, "Whale with harness could be Russian weapon, say Norwegian experts," The Guardian, April 29, 2019

13 Hopkins, C. J., "The War on White Supremacist Terror," Consent Factory, August 8, 2019

14 Douglas, Lawrence, "Do the Brazil Amazon fires justify environmental interventionism?" The Guardian, August 31, 2019

"our house is burning,"[15] and our world is on fire,[16] and there are "concentration camps,"[17] and a "coup in Great Britain"[18] ... or whatever ass-puckering apocalyptic panic the global capitalist ruling classes determine they need to foment that day, we will know that this news has been algorithmically vetted and approved by DARPA and its corporate, academic, and government partners, and thus, is absolutely "real" and "true," or we wouldn't be seeing it on the screen of our devices.

If you think this vision is science fiction, or dystopian satire, think again. Or read this recent article in *Bloomberg*, "U.S. Unleashes Military to Fight Fake News, Disinformation."[19] Here's the lede to get you started ...

> "Fake news and social media posts are such a threat to U.S. security that the Defense Department is launching a project to repel 'large-scale, automated disinformation attacks' ... the Defense Advanced Research Projects Agency (DARPA) wants custom software that can unearth fakes hidden among more than 500,000 stories, photos, video and audio clips. If successful, the system after four years of trials may expand to detect malicious intent and prevent viral fake news from polarizing society ..."

What could be more reassuring than the knowledge that DARPA and its corporate partners will be scanning the entire Internet for content created with "malicious intent," or which has the potential to "polarize" society, and making sure we never see that stuff? If they can't do it, I don't know who can. They developed the Internet, after all. I'm not exactly sure how they did it, but Yasha Levine wrote a book about it, which I think we're still technically allowed to read.[20]

---

15 Emmanuel Macron on Twitter, August 22, 2019 ("Our house is burning. Literally. The Amazon rain forest - the lungs which produces 20% of our planet's oxygen - is on fire.")

16 Black, Catte, "Amazon Burning? – well maybe not so much," OffGuardian, August 23, 2019 ("Statistics indicate this is an average year for wildfires, so why the above-average hysteria?")

17 Johnson, Benny, "Here Are The Photos Of Obama's Illegal Immigrant Detention Facilities The Media Won't Show You," Daily Caller, June 19, 2019

18 Van Wagtendonk, Anya, "UK protesters denounce 'coup' after Boris Johnson shuts down Parliament," Vox, August 31, 2019

19 Norman, Pete, "U.S. Unleashes Military to Fight Fake News, Disinformation," Bloomberg News, August 31, 2019

20 Surveillance Valley by Yasha Levine, Public Affairs, 2018

Anyway, according to the *Bloomberg* article, DARPA and its corporate partners won't have the system up and running in time for the 2020 elections, so the Putin-Nazis will probably win again. Which means we are looking at four more years of relentless Russia and fascism hysteria, and fake-news and divisive-content hysteria, and anti-Semitism and racism hysteria, and ... well, basically, general apocalyptic panic over anything and everything you can possibly think of.

Believe me, I know, that prospect is exhausting ... but the global capitalist ruling classes need to keep everyone whipped up into a shrieking apoplectic frenzy over anything other than global capitalism until they can win the War on Populism and globally implement the New Normality, after which the really serious reality policing can finally begin.

I don't know, call me crazy, or a Person of Malicious Intent, but I think I'd prefer that boot in the face.

Trumpenstein Must Be Destroyed!

October 4, 2019

So, here we go … like a 1960s straight-to-drive-in Hammer Film Production, the 2020 campaign season has begun. Dig into your bucket of popcorn, pop the flap on your box of Good & Plenty, turn off your mind, and enjoy the show. From the looks of the trailer, it's going to be a doozy.

That's right, folks, it's the final installment of the popular Trumpenstein horror movie series, TRUMPENSTEIN MUST BE DESTROYED! It will be playing, more or less around the clock, on more or less every screen in existence, until November 3, 2020 … or until Trump takes that lonely walk across the White House lawn to the Marine One chopper and flies off to Mar-a-Lago in disgrace.

Here's a quick recap of the series so far, for those who may be joining us late.

When we last saw Trumpenstein he was out on the balcony of the White House South Portico in his Brioni boxers, ripped to the gills on Diet Coke and bellowing like a bull elephant seal. Having narrowly survived the Resistance's attempts to expose him as a Russian intelligence asset (and the reanimated corpse of Adolf Hitler), he was pounding his chest and hollering angry gibberish at the liberal media like the Humongous in the second *Mad Max* movie.

The liberal mob was standing around with their torches and pitchforks in a state of shock. Doctor Mueller, the "monster hunter," had let Trumpenstein slip through his fingers. The supposedly ironclad case against him had turned out to be a bunch of lies made up by the Intelligence community, the Democratic Party, and the corporate media.

Russiagate was officially dead. The President of the United States was not a Russian secret agent. No one was blackmailing anyone with a videotape of Romanian prostitutes peeing on a bed where

Obama once slept. All that had happened was, millions of liberals had been subjected to the most elaborate psyop in the history of elaborate deep state psyops ... which, ironically, had only further strengthened Trumpenstein, who was out there on the Portico balcony, shotgunning Diet Cokes with one hand and shaking his junk at the mob with the other.

It wasn't looking so good for "democracy."

Fortunately, even though Russiagate had blown up in the Resistance's faces and Trumpenstein could no longer be painted as a traitorous Russian intelligence asset (or Vladimir Putin's homosexual lover[1]), he was still the reanimated corpse of Hitler, so they went balls out on the fascism hysteria, which kept the Resistance alive through the summer.

Which was all they really needed to do. Because these last three years were basically just a warm-up for the main event, which was always scheduled to begin this autumn. Russiagate, Hitlergate, and all the rest of it ... it was all just a prelude to these impeachment hearings, and to the mass hysteria surrounding same, which the global capitalist ruling classes, the Intelligence community, and the corporate media will be barraging us with until November 2020. The details don't really matter that much. They were always going to impeach him for something, and they were always going to do it now, and throughout the 2020 campaign season.

You do not honestly believe they are going to let him serve a second term, do you? He took them by surprise in 2016. That isn't going to happen again. Seriously, take a moment and reflect on everything we've been subjected to since Hillary Clinton lost the election ... the unmitigated insanity of it all. The Russiagate hysteria. The Russian hacker hysteria. The Russian Facebook mind-control hysteria. The Hitler hysteria. The mass fascism hysteria. Anti-Semitism hysteria. Concentration camp hysteria. White supremacist terrorism hysteria. Russian spy whales. Perfume assassins. The endless stream of fabricated "news" stories pumped out by the corporate media. Best-selling

---

1 "Trump and Putin - A Love Story," one of a series of three short video cartoons that combine real Donald Trump audio clips with hand-drawn fantasy animations by Bill Plympton, produced by Billy Shebar and David Roberts of 110th Street Films (video available online at https://110th-street.com)

books, based on nothing. Comedians singing hymns to former FBI directors on national television. Celebrities demanding CIA coups. Papers of record like *The New York Times* coordinating blatant propaganda campaigns.

The list goes on, and on, and on.

All of this because one billionaire ass clown won an election without their permission?

No, this was never just about Donald Trump, repulsive and corrupt as the man may be. The stakes have always been much higher than that. What we've witnessed over the the last three years (and what is about to reach its apogee) is a global capitalist counter-insurgency, the goal of which is (a) to put down the ongoing populist rebellion throughout the West, and (b) to crush any hope of resistance to the hegemony of global capitalism ... in other words, a War on Populism.

Not that Donald Trump is a populist hero. Far from it. Trump is a narcissistic clown. He has always been a narcissistic clown. All he really cares about is seeing his face on television and plastering his name on everything in sight, preferably in huge gold letters. He got himself elected president by being cunning enough to recognize and ride the tsunami of populist anger that was building up in 2016, and that has continued to build throughout his presidency.

It is not going away, that anger. The Western masses are no more thrilled about the global capitalist future today than they were when they voted for Brexit, and Trump, and various other "populist" and reactionary figures.

Which is precisely why Trumpenstein must be destroyed, and why Brexit must not be allowed to happen ... or, if it does, why the people of the United Kingdom must be mercilessly punished. It is also why the Gilets Jaunes are being brutally repressed by the French police, and disappeared by the corporate media (while the Hong Kong protesters garner daily headlines), and why Jeremy Corbyn and the Labour Party must be smeared as a hive of anti-Semites, and Tulsi Gabbard as an Assad-apologist, and why Julian Assange must be smeared and destroyed, and why Bernie Sanders must also be destroyed, and why anyone of any ilk (left, right, it doesn't matter) riding that wave of populist anger or challenging the hegemony of global capitalism and its psychotic, smiley-face ideology in any other way must be destroyed.

2020 is for all the marbles. The global capitalist ruling classes either crush this ongoing populist insurgency or … God knows where we go from here.

Try to see it through their eyes for a moment. Picture four more years of Trump … second-term Trump … Trump unleashed. Do you really believe they're going to let that happen, that they are going to permit this populist insurgency to continue for another four years?

They are not. What they are going to do is use all their power to destroy the monster … not Trump the man, but Trump the symbol. They are going to drown us in impeachment minutiae, drip, drip, drip, for the next twelve months. The liberal corporate media are going to go full-Goebbels. They are going to whip up so much mass hysteria that people won't be able to think. They are going to pit us one against the other, and force us onto one or the other side of a simulated conflict (Democracy versus the Putin-Nazis) to keep us from perceiving the actual conflict (Global Capitalism versus Populism). They are going to bring us to the brink of civil war in order to prevent civil war. And, if that doesn't work, and Trump gets reelected (or if it looks like he's going to get reelected), they'll probably have to just go ahead and kill him.

One way or another, this is it.

This is the part where the global capitalist ruling classes teach us all a lesson. The lesson they intend to teach us is the same old lesson that masters have been teaching slaves since the dawn of slavery. The lesson is, "abandon hope." The lesson is, "resistance is futile." The lesson is, "shut up, eat your tofu, get back to work at your three gig jobs, service your school loans and your credit card debt, vote for who and what we tell you, and be grateful we don't fucking kill you. Oh, yeah … and if you want to rebel against something, feel free to take up identity politics, or to march around town with posters of Saint Greta demanding that we stop destroying the planet. We'll get right on that, don't you worry."

What? You thought this had a happy ending, that Trumpenstein and the Bride of Trumpenstein were going to ride off into the orange sunrise at Mar-a-Lago in a Trump-branded golf cart, having made America great again … or that Bernie was going to storm the castle, vanquish Trumpenstein, and set up something resembling basic social democracy?

I told you it was a horror film, didn't I?

Reclaiming Your Inner Fascist

November 19, 2019

OK, we need to talk about fascism. Not just any kind of fascism. A particularly insidious kind of fascism. No, not the fascism of the early 20th Century. Not Mussolini's National Fascist Party. Not Hitler's NSDAP. Not Francoist fascism or any other kind of organized fascist movement or party. Not even the dreaded Tiki-Torch Nazis.

It's the other kind of fascism we need to talk about. The kind that doesn't come goose-stepping up the street waving big neo-Nazi flags. The kind we don't recognize when we're looking right at it.

It's like that joke about the fish and the water … we don't recognize it because we're swimming in it. We're surrounded by it. We are inseparable from it. From the moment we are born, we breathe it in.

We are taught it by our parents, who were taught it by their parents. We are taught it again by our teachers in school. It is reinforced on a daily basis at work, in conversations with friends, in our families and our romantic relationships. We imbibe it in books, movies, TV shows, advertisements, pop songs, the nightly news, in our cars, at the mall, the stadium, the opera … everywhere, because it is literally everywhere.

It doesn't look like fascism to us. Fascism only looks like fascism when you're standing outside of it, or looking back at it. When you are in it, fascism just looks like "normality," like "reality," like "just the way it is."

We (i.e., Americans, Brits, Europeans, and other citizens of the global capitalist empire) get up in the morning, go to work, shop, pay the interest on our debts, and otherwise obey the laws and conform to the mores of a system of power that has murdered countless millions of people in pursuit of global hegemonic dominance. It has perpetrated numerous wars of aggression. Its military occupies most of the planet. Its Intelligence agencies (i.e., secret police) operate a worldwide surveillance apparatus that can identify, target, and eliminate anyone, anywhere, often by remote control. Its propaganda network never sleeps, nor is there any real way to escape its constant emotional and ideological conditioning.

The fact that the global capitalist empire does not call itself an empire (or a "Reich"), and, instead, calls itself "democracy," doesn't make it any less of an empire. The fact that it uses terms like "regime change" instead of "invasion" or "annexation" makes very little difference to its victims. Terms like "security," "stability," "intervention," "regime change," and so on are not meant for its victims. They are meant for us … to anesthetize us.

The empire is "regime-changing" Bolivia currently. It has "regime-changed" most of Latin America at one time or another since the Second World War. It "regime-changed" Iraq, Libya, Yugoslavia, Indonesia … the list goes on. It very much wants to "regime-change" Iran, which it "regime-changed" back in the 1950s, before the Iranians "regime-changed" it back. It would love to "regime-change" Russia and China, but their ICBMs make that somewhat impractical. Basically, the empire has been "regime-changing" everyone it can since the end of the Cold War. It has run into a little bump in Syria, and in Venezuela, but not to worry, it will get back there and finish up eventually.

Now, let's be clear about this "regime-change" business. We're talking about invading other people's countries, and orchestrating and sponsoring coups, or otherwise overthrowing their governments, and murdering, torturing, and oppressing people. Sending in terrorists, death squads, and such. We have organizations that train guys to do that, i.e., to round people up, take them out to the jungle, or the woods, or wherever, rape the women, and then summarily shoot everyone in the head.[1] We pay for this kind of thing with our taxes, and our investments in the global corporations that our militaries and intelligence agencies serve.

We know this is happening. We can google this stuff. We know "where the trains are going," as it were.

And yet, we do not see ourselves as monsters.

---

1 Sprague, Jeb, "Top Bolivian coup plotters trained by US military's School of the Americas, served as attachés in FBI police programs," The Grayzone, November 13, 2019

The Nazis didn't see themselves as monsters. They saw themselves as heroes, as saviors, or just as regular Germans leading regular lives. When they looked at the propaganda posters which surrounded them (as the Internet surrounds us today), they didn't see sadistic mass-murderers and totalitarian psychopathic freaks. They saw normal people, admirable people, who were making the world a better place. They saw themselves.

They saw "the good guys."

This is primarily how propaganda works. It isn't meant to fool anybody. It is there to represent "normality" (whatever "normality" happens to be in whatever empire one happens to inhabit). It is Power's way of letting us know what it wants us to believe, how it wants us to behave, who our official enemies are. Its purpose isn't to mislead or deceive us. It is an edict, a command, an ideological model … to which we are all expected to conform. Conform to this ideological model, and one is rewarded, or at least not punished. Deviate from it, and suffer the consequences.

It is a question of obedience, not one of truth.

This is why it doesn't matter that there is no actual "Attack on America," and that the Russians didn't "hack," "subvert," "meddle in," or otherwise significantly "influence" the 2016 presidential election or otherwise put Donald Trump in office. John Brennan and the CIA say they did,[2] and the corporate media say they did, so all Good Americans have to pretend to believe it.

Likewise, it also doesn't matter if an organization like the OPCW collaborated with the empire's regime-change specialists who staged a "chemical weapons attack"[3] on helpless women and children in Douma (because, no matter what the empire did or didn't do, Assad

---

2 Maté, Aaron, "The Brennan Dossier: All About a Prime Mover of Russiagate," Real Clear Investigations, November 15, 2019 ("The January 2017 report, called an Intelligence Community Assessment, followed months of leaks to the media that had falsely suggested illicit ties between the Trump campaign and the Kremlin while also revealing that such contacts were the subject of a federal investigation. Its release cast a pall of suspicion over Trump just days before he took office, setting the tone for the unfounded allegations of conspiracy and treason that have engulfed his first term. The ICA's blockbuster finding was presented to the public as the consensus view of the nation's intelligence community. As events have unfolded, however, it now seems apparent that the report was largely the work of one agency, the CIA, and overseen by one man, then-Director John Brennan, who closely directed its drafting and publication with a small group of hand-picked analysts.")

3 Johnstone, Caitlin, "Panel Finds Gaping Holes in OPCW Report on Alleged Syrian Chemical Attack," Consortium News, October 25, 2019

is a Russian-backed, baby-gassing devil!), or if *The Guardian* just makes up stuff about Julian Assange out of whole cloth and prints it as news.[4]

This is also why, when *The Guardian* prints an enormous color propaganda photo of a beneficent-looking Hillary Clinton and her soon-to-be-Democratic senator daughter posing as our last line of defense against the Imminent Invasion of the Putin-Nazis, and as the future of Western democracy, and whatever, on the cover of its cultural *Review*,[5] this isn't perceived as propaganda. Never mind that this woman (i.e., Hillary) is directly responsible for the deaths and misery of God knows how many innocent people in the course of her lucrative service to the empire. Never mind that this is the same exact person that sadistically cackled on national television when the empire's associates anally knife-raped and murdered Muammar Gaddafi in Libya, and then transformed a developed African country into a hellish human-slavery market.[6]

For fascists (and authoritarian personalities generally), facts are completely beside the point. The point is to robotically conform to the ideology (or hysterical ravings) of whatever leader or system of power happens to be in charge of things.

Authoritarian personality types are skilled at determining exactly who that is (i.e., who is really in charge of things) and obsequiously currying favor with them. For some, this is an innate talent; others have this talent conditioned into them (or beaten into them) over the course of years. Either way, the result is the same.

Put a bunch of random people together in a group and give them a problem to solve, or a complex project or objective to accomplish. Don't give them any organizational guidance, just put them in a room and watch what happens.

The first thing that happens is … a "leader" emerges. Someone (or a few people) decides that someone needs to be in charge of this project, and they feel pretty strongly that it should be them.

---

4 Greenwald, Glenn, "Five Weeks After The Guardian's Viral Blockbuster Assange-Manafort Scoop, No Evidence Has Emerged — Just Stonewalling," The Intercept, January 2, 2019

5 Higgins, Charlotte, "Hillary and Chelsea Clinton: 'We cannot give in. That's how they win'" The Guardian Review, November 16, 2019

6 Nebehay, Stephanie, "Executions, torture and slave markets persist in Libya: U.N.," Reuters, March 21, 2018

If more than one such "leader" emerges, or if the need for a leader itself is challenged, a struggle for power will immediately ensue. The aspiring "leaders" will compete for the support of the "followers" in the group. Sides will be taken. Eventually, a leader will be chosen. Occasionally, this will happen openly, but, more often than not, it will happen unconsciously. Someone in the group will want to dominate ... and the rest of the group will want them to dominate. They will experience discomfort until a leader is established, and they will feel an enormous sense of relief once one is, and they can surrender their autonomy.

I assume you're familiar with the Milgram experiment, but, if not, you should probably read up on that, and maybe read Adorno's *The Authoritarian Personality*.[7] It's a bit outdated, and over-focused on the Nazis (it was originally published in 1950), but I think you'll get the general idea.

Once you've done that, turn on your television, or your radio, or scan the news on the Internet, or walk down any big city street and compare the content on the digital billboards, movie posters, and advertisements to historical fascist propaganda ... that is, if your boss will let you leave the workplace long enough to do that, which he probably will if you ask him in that special way you have learned over time that he likes and generally tends to respond to.

Sorry ... I didn't mean to get inside your mind. That's kind of a fascistic thing to do.

Look, the point is, we all have an "Inner Fascist," with whom we are either acquainted or not. I'm a playwright and a novelist, which means I've got a big, fat, Sieg-heiling Inner Fascist goose-stepping around inside my head. I invent whole worlds, which I dictatorially control. I put people in them and make them say things. It doesn't get much more fascistic than that.

The way I see it, my art is how I sublimate my Inner Fascist, so that he doesn't run around invading Poland, exterminating the Jews, or "regime-changing" Bolivia.

I'm not a psychiatrist, or a fascism expert, but I figure this is probably the most we can do ... recognize, acknowledge, and find some

7 Adorno, Theodor, Frenkel-Brunswik, Else, Levinson, Daniel J., and Sanford, R. Nevitt, The Authoritarian Personality, Harper & Brothers, 1950

way to sublimate our Inner Fascists, because, I guarantee you, they're not going away. (If you don't believe me, go watch that *Planet Earth* episode featuring the fascist chimpanzees.)

Seriously, I recommend you do this. Get acquainted with your Inner Fascist, in an appropriate set and setting, of course. Give him something safe to dominate and then let him go totally totalitarian.

You'll be doing yourself and the rest of us a favor.

Ironically, it is those who are not acquainted with their Inner Fascists (or who adamantly deny that they have one) who are usually the first to make a big public show of loudly denouncing "fascism," brandishing their "anti-fascist" bona fides, accusing other people of being "fascists," and otherwise desperately projecting their Inner Fascists onto those they hate, and want to silence, if not exterminate.

This is one of the hallmarks of repressed Inner Fascism … this compulsion to control what other people think, this desire for complete ideological conformity, this tendency, not to argue with, but rather, to attempt to destroy anyone who disagrees with or questions one's beliefs.

We all know people who behave this way. If you don't, odds are, one of them is you.

So, please, if you haven't done so already, get acquainted with your Inner Fascist, and find him something harmless to do, before he … well, you know, starts singing hymns to former FBI directors,[8] or worshipping the CIA,[9] or Obama, or Trump, or Hillary Clinton, or supports the empire's next invasion, or coup, or just makes a desperate, sanctimonious ass of you both on the Internet.

I'm not kidding. Reclaim your Inner Fascist.

It might sound crazy, but you will thank me someday.

---

8 Upadhyaya, Kayla Kumari, "Women of 'SNL' Sing 'All I Want for Christmas Is You' to Robert Mueller," Hollywood Reporter, December 1, 2018

9 John Krasinski, speaking at a publicity event for the 2018 Hollywood movie Tom Clancy's Jack Ryan ("The CIA is something that we should all not only cherish, but be saying thank you for every single day." See, https://twitter.com/dewybleach/status/1196628293103079424)

The Year of Manufactured Hysteria

December 18, 2019

Well, it looks like we've somehow managed to survive another year of diabolical Putin-Nazi attacks on democracy. It was touch-and-go there for a while, especially coming down the home stretch, what with Jeremy Corbyn's desperate attempt to overthrow the UK government, construct a British version of Auschwitz, and start rounding up and mass-murdering the Jews.[1]

That was certainly pretty scary … but then, the whole year was pretty scary.

The horror began promptly in early January, when Rachel Maddow revealed that Putin was projecting words out of Trump's mouth in real-time, i.e., literally using Trump's head like a puppet, or one of those *Mission Impossible* masks.[2] And that was just the tip of the iceberg, as, despite the best efforts of Integrity Initiative,[3] Bellingcat,[4] and other such establishment psyops,[5] Internet-censoring websites like NewsGuard,[6] and an army of mass-hysteria generators,[7] Putin's

---

1 "Reopening Auschwitz – The Conspiracy To Stop Corbyn," Media Lens, December 3, 2019

2 Maddow, Rachel, "Trump curiously well versed in specific Russian talking points," MSNBC, January 4, 2019

3 Blumenthal, Max and Ames, Mark, "Covert British military-intelligence smear machine is meddling in American politics, documents reveal," The Grayzone, January 8, 2019

4 James, Steve, "The Bellingcat research collective: War propaganda masquerading as 'citizen journalism'," World Socialist Website, October 13, 2016

5 Webb, Whitney, "Omidyar's Intercept Teams Up with War-Propaganda Firm Bellingcat," Mint Press News, October 8, 2018

6 Li, Kenneth, "NewsGuard's 'real news' seal of approval helps spark change in fake news era," Reuters, February 1, 2019

7 Coppins, McKay, "How the Left Lost Its Mind," The Atlantic, July 2, 2017 ("The Trump era has given rise to a vast alternative left-wing media infrastructure that operates largely out of the view of casual news consumers, but commands a massive audience and growing influence in liberal America. There are polemical podcasters and partisan click farms; wild-eyed conspiracists and cynical fabulists. Some traffic heavily in rumor and wage campaigns of misinformation; others are merely aggregators and commentators who have carved out a corner of the web for themselves. But taken together, they form a media universe where partisan hysteria is too easily stoked, and fake news can travel at the speed of light.")

legion of Russian "influencers" was continuing to maliciously influence Americans, who were probably also under attack by brain-eating Russian-Cubano crickets![8]

While Resistance members were still wrapping their heads in anti-cricket aluminum foil, Putin (i.e., Russian Hitler) ordered Trump (i.e., Russian-asset Hitler) to launch a coup in Venezuela (i.e., Russian Hitler's South American ally), probably to distract us from "Smirkboy Hitler"[9] and his acne-faced gang of MAGA cap-wearing Catholic high-school Hitler Youth, who were trying to invade and Hitlerize the capital.

Or maybe the coup was meant to distract us from the un-American activities of Bernie Sanders, who had also been exposed as a Russian asset, or a devious "Kremlin-Trump operation,"[10] or was working with Tulsi Gabbard to build an army of blood-drinking Hindu nationalists, genocidal Assadists, and American fascists[11] to help the Iranians (and the Russians, of course, and presumably also Jeremy Corbyn) frontally assault the State of Israel and drive the Jews into the sea.

As if all that wasn't horrifying enough (and ridiculous and confusing enough), by early Spring there was mounting evidence that Putin had somehow gotten to Mueller, possibly with one of those FSB pee-tapes, and was sabotaging the "Russiagate" coup the Intelligence community, the Democratic Party, the corporate media, and the rest of the Resistance had been methodically preparing since 2016. Liberals' anuses began puckering and unpuckering as it gradually became clear that the "Mueller Report" was not going to prove that Donald Trump had colluded with Putin and Julian Assange to steal the presidency from Hillary Clinton and transform the United States of America into a genocidal Putin-Nazi Reich.

---

8 Greenwald, Glenn, "NBC and MSNBC Blamed Russia for Using 'Sophisticated Microwaves' to Cause 'Brain Injuries' in U.S. 'Diplomats' in Cuba. The Culprits Were Likely Crickets." The Intercept, January 7, 2019

9 Holmes, Dave, "I Saw the Smirk With My Eyes, But Felt It in My Gut," Esquire, January 22, 2019

10 Virginia Heffernan, professional journalist, on Twitter, January 26, 2019 ("A thread about the possibility of Bernie Sanders as a very 2016 Kremlin-Trump operation")

11 Rao, Shrenik, "Tulsi Gabbard Unites Putin Apologists, Bloodstained Modi, Genocidal Assad and the U.S. Far Right," Haaretz, October 19, 2019

Meanwhile, the anti-Semitism pandemic[12] that had mysteriously erupted in 2016 (i.e., right around the time Trump won the nomination) was raging unchecked throughout the West. Jews in Great Britain were on the brink of panic because approximately 0.08 percent of Labour Party members were anti-Semitic,[13] as opposed to the rest of the British public, who have never shown any signs of anti-Semitism (or any other kind of racism or bigotry), and are practically a nation of Shabbos goys. Clearly, Corbyn had turned the party into his personal neo-Nazi death cult[14] and was planning to carry out a second Holocaust just as soon as he renationalized the British railways!

And it wasn't just the United Kingdom. According to corporate media virologists, idiopathic anti-Semitism was breaking out everywhere. In France, the "Yellow Vests" were also anti-Semites.[15] In the USA, Jews were facing "a perfect storm of anti-Semitism," some of it stemming from the neo-fascist fringe (which has been a part of the American landscape forever, but which the corporate media has elevated into an international Nazi movement), but much of it whipped up by Ilhan Omar,[16] who had apparently entered into a "Red-Brown" pact with Richard Spencer, or Gavin McInnes, or some other formerly insignificant idiot.

Things got very confusing for a while, as Republicans united with Democrats to denounce Ilhan Omar as an anti-Semite (and possibly a full-fledged Islamic terrorist), and to condemn the existence of "hate," or whatever. The corporate media, Facebook, and Twitter were suddenly swarming with hordes of angry anti-Semites accusing other anti-Semites of anti-Semitism. Meghan McCain couldn't take it anymore, and she broke down on the Joy Behar Show and begged to be converted to Judaism, or Zionism, right there on the air.[17] This

12 *Hopkins, C. J., "Anti-Semitism Pandemic!" Consent Factory, March 11, 2019*

13 *Knightly, Kit, "Anti-Capitalism is NOT Anti-Semitism," OffGuardian, March 5, 2019*

14 *Cohen, Roger, "Jeremy Corbyn's Anti-Semitic Labour Party," The New York Times, February 28, 2019*

15 *Vandoorne, Saskya, "Yellow Vest protesters fan flames of anti-Semitism in France," CNN, March 9, 2019*

16 *Kerstein, Benjamin, "Ilhan Omar and the Axis of Antisemitism," The Algemeiner, March 10, 2019*

17 *The View, ABC, March 7, 2019*

unseemly display of anti-anti-Semitism was savagely skewered by Eli Valley, an "anti-Semitic" Jewish cartoonist, according to McCain and other morons.[18]

Then it happened ... perhaps the loudest popcorn fart in political history. The Mueller Report was finally delivered. And just like that, Russiagate was over. After three long years of manufactured mass hysteria, corporate media propaganda, books, T-shirts, marches, etc., Robert Mueller had come up with squat. Zip. Zero. Nichts. Nada. No collusion. No pee-tape. No secret servers. No Russian contacts. Nothing. Zilch.

Cognitive dissonance gripped the nation. There was beaucoup wailing and gnashing of teeth. Resistance members doubled their anti-depressant dosages and went into mourning. Shell-shocked liberals did their best to pretend they hadn't been duped, again, by authoritative sources like *The Washington Post*, *The New York Times*, *The Guardian*, CNN, MSNBC, et al., which had disseminated completely fabricated stories about secret meetings which never took place, power grid hackings that never happened, Russian servers that never existed, imaginary Russian propaganda peddlers, and the list goes on, and on, and on[19] ... and hadn't otherwise behaved like a bunch of mindless, shrieking neo-McCarthyites.

Except that Russiagate wasn't over. It immediately morphed into "Obstructiongate." As the corporate media spooks explained, Mueller's investigation of Trump was never about collusion with Russia. No, it was always about Trump obstructing the investigation of the collusion with Russia that the investigation was not about, and that everyone knew had never happened.[20]

In other words, Mueller's investigation was launched in order to investigate the obstruction of his investigation.

---

18 Staff, Toi and Agencies, "Meghan McCain raps anti-Semitism, gets 'anti-Semitic' treatment by Jewish artist," Times of Israel, March 10, 2019 ("Emotional criticism by Meghan McCain of Democrat Congresswoman Ilhan Omar's allegedly anti-Semitic remarks has spawned an online uproar, after [Eli Valley] a Jewish artist drew a cartoon that mocked the late Arizona senator's daughter and was himself accused of employing anti-Semitic tropes and imagery.")

19 Greenwald, Glenn, "Beyond BuzzFeed: The 10 Worst, Most Embarrassing U.S. Media Failures on the Trump-Russia Story," The Intercept, January 20, 2019

20 Taibbi, Matt, "'Corroboration Zero': An Inspector General's Report Reveals the Steele Dossier Was Always a Joke," Rolling Stone, December 10, 2019

Or whatever. It didn't really matter, because, by this time, Assange had been arrested for treason, or for jumping bail, or for smearing poo all over the walls of the Ecuadorean embassy, and *The New York Times* was reporting that a veritable "constellation" of social media accounts "linked to Russia and far-right groups" was disseminating extremist "disinformation," [21] and Putin had unleashed the Russian spy whale,[22] and "Jews were not safe in Germany again,"[23] because the Putin-Nazis had formed an alliance with the Iranian Nazis and the Syrian Nazis, who were backing the Palestinian Nazis that Antifa was fighting on behalf of Israel,[24] and Jews were not safe in the UK either, because of Jeremy Corbyn, who Donald Trump (who, let's all remember, is literally Hitler) was conspiring with a group of "unnamed Jewish leaders" to prevent from becoming prime minister, and Iran was conspiring with Hezbollah and al Qaeda[25] to amass an arsenal of WMDs to launch at Israel and Saudi Arabia, and other peaceful Middle Eastern democracies, and Trump was finally going to go full-Hitler and declare martial law on the Fourth of July, and he was operating literal "concentration camps" where immigrants were "being forced to drink out of toilets,"[26] which looked almost exactly the same as the "detention facilities" Obama had operated,[27] except for ... well, you know, the "fascism." So who had time to worry about the corporate media colluding with an attempted Intelligence community coup?

Then, in August, right on cue, some racist whack job murdered a bunch of people, and so now, as if the mass hysteria hadn't already

21 Apuzzo, Matt and Satariano, Adam, "Europe, 'Russia Is Targeting Europe's Elections. So Are Far-Right Copycats,'" The New York Times, May 12, 2019

22 Ellis-Peterson, Hannah, "Whale with harness could be Russian weapon, say Norwegian experts," The Guardian, April 29, 2019

23 Schuetze, Christopher F., "Amid Rising Anti-Semitism, German Official Advises Jews Against Wearing Skullcaps in Public," The New York Times, May 26, 2019

24 Hopkins, C. J., "The Quds Day Panic of 2019," Consent Factory, June 5, 2019

25 McKay, Hollie, "More evidence emerges of Iran-Al Qaeda ties," FOX News, May 8, 2019

26 Rennix, Brianna and Robinson, Nathan, "Crammed into cells and forced to drink from the toilet – this is how the US treats migrants," The Guardian, July 3, 2019 (The "toilets" in question were the standard metal all-in-one units featured in most prisons and detention centers, in which the toilet is below and the sink is above.)

27 Johnson, Benny, "Here Are The Photos Of Obama's Illegal Immigrant Detention Facilities The Media Won't Show You," Daily Caller, June 19, 2019 (The photos are indistinguishable from the detention facilities used by the Trump administration.)

been jacked up to the max, America had "a white nationalist terrorist problem," or was in the throes of a "white nationalist terrorism crisis."[28] Trump was now officially "Nihilist in Chief,"[29] and "a white supremacist who inspires terrorism,"[30] and was basically no different than Anwar al-Awlaki.[31] So it was time to take some extraordinary measures along the lines of the Patriot Act, except focused on potential white supremacist terrorists, or anyone the Editorial Board of *The New York Times* might deem a "threat."[32]

This sudden outbreak of "Trump-inspired terrorism"[33] and the manufactured "fascism" hysteria that followed got the Resistance through the end of the Summer and into the Autumn, which was always when the main event was scheduled to begin. See, these last three years have basically been a warm-up for what is about to happen … the impeachment, sure, but that's only one part of it.

If you thought the global capitalist ruling classes and the corporate media's methodical crushing of Jeremy Corbyn[34] was depressing to watch … well, prepare yourself for 2020.

The Year of Manufactured Mass Hysteria was not just the US Intelligence community and the corporate media getting their kicks by whipping the public up into an endless series of baseless panics over imaginary Russians and Nazis. It was the final phase of cementing the official "Putin-Nazi" narrative in people's minds.

For the sake of anyone new to my columns, here's how the Putin-Nazi narrative works …

---

28 Werlman, C. J., "US in the midst of a white nationalist terrorism crisis," The Sydney Morning Herald, August 4, 2019

29 Douthat, Ross, "The Nihilist in Chief," The New York Times, August 6, 2019

30 Soufan, Ali H., "I Spent 25 Years Fighting Jihadis. White Supremacists Aren't So Different," The New York Times, August 5, 2019

31 McQuade, Barbara, "A Charismatic Leader for White Nationalists," The Atlantic, August 6, 2019

32 The Editorial Board, "We Have a White Nationalist Terrorist Problem," The New York Times, August 5, 2019

33 Schanzer, David, "We must call the El Paso shooting what it is: Trump-inspired terrorism," The Guardian, August 5, 2019

34 Norton, Ben and Blumenthal, Max, "Russiagate media smears against Corbyn brought to you by US and UK military-intelligence apparatus," The Grayzone, December 8, 2019 ("Days before Britain's historic election, the UK's military-intelligence apparatus is turning to the corporate media and US government-funded NATO cut-outs to smear Labour leader Jeremy Corbyn with evidence-free Russiagate allegations.")

The Putin-Nazi narrative has two basic parts, or messages, which are constantly repeated: (1) "Russia is attacking our democracy!" and (2) "Fascism is spreading like wildfire!," both of which are essentially fictions.

This official Putin-Nazi narrative was introduced in the Summer of 2016, and replaced the official "War on Terror" narrative, which had run for fifteen years, and which was just as fictional. It has been methodically reinforced and repeated by the neoliberal establishment, the corporate media (and, more recently, the alternative media, and even by extremely intelligent anarchist anthropologists like David Graeber[35]) for the last three years on a daily basis. At this point it has become our "reality," just as the War on Terror became our "reality" ... as the Cold War had previously been our "reality."

When I say this narrative has become our "reality," I mean that it is now virtually impossible to refute it in any mainstream forum without being dismissed as a "conspiracy theorist," or an "anti-Semite," or a "Russian asset." It has become axiomatic and is taken for granted that we are experiencing an explosion of anti-Semitism, and fascism, and that Russia is out to get us (so axiomatic that someone like Graeber falls into the trap of defending Corbyn by relying on, and thus reifying, the very "fascism" hysteria that was used to destroy him).

Never mind that the entire planet continues to be ruled by global capitalism, transnational corporations, and supragovernmental bodies, and that most of it is occupied by the US military, NATO, and other GloboCap allies, and assorted corporate military contractors. Never mind that Russia isn't "attacking" anyone, and that the "Nazis" haven't taken over anything, and that no one is rounding up and murdering the Jews, or the Mexicans, or anyone else for that matter ... because when have facts had anything to do with maintaining an official narrative?

The answer, in case you were wondering, is "never." We are, all of us, living in a fiction. A fiction authored by those in power to serve the interests of those in power. That's what an official narrative is.

---

35 David Graeber on Twitter, December 3, 2019 Video ("This video is going up in a bunch of places but here's mine: my take on the Anti-Semitism controversy and why intentionally fanning the flames, as so many are doing, endangers Jewish people.")

It makes no difference whether we believe it or not. It functions as "reality" regardless. If you doubt that ... well, just ask Jeremy Corbyn. Or watch as the Labour "anti-Semitism crisis" abruptly evaporates into thin air, as the War on Terror did in 2016, once it no longer served a useful purpose.

As for 2020, I'm afraid the manufactured mass hysteria is only going to get worse. The global capitalist ruling classes are determined to snuff out this populist rebellion, and to make sure it never happens again, or at the very least not on this scale. Anyone who gets in the way is going to be branded an "anti-Semite," or a "fascist," or a "Russian asset." Politicians who do not toe the line are going to have their political careers and personal reputations destroyed. (Did you notice how it took less than two days after the crushing of Jeremy Corbyn for the smearing of Sanders as an anti-Semite or "soft on anti-Semitism" to begin?[36])

Mainstream journalists who dare to question the official Putin-Nazi narrative, even in the most respectful way, are going to come under increasing pressure to tone it down or suffer the consequences.

Putin-Nazi paranoia will metastasize. Dissident websites will be deplatformed and demonetized. The Internet will be increasingly monitored for any and all forms of nonconformity. Dissent will be increasingly stigmatized.

"Reality" will be increasingly policed.

It's all going to get extremely unpleasant, and that's assuming that civil war doesn't break out.

And as for me, I'm just a political satirist with a barely respectable cult-sized following, so they'll probably let me get away with continuing to cover the whole ugly show (as long as no one starts to take me seriously). I'll try to find the humor in it, but honestly, just between you and me, what's coming may not be all that funny.

---

36 Hoffman, Ari, "What The US Left Should Learn From Jeremy Corbyn's Shellacking," Forward, December 13, 2019 ("The benefits of Corbyn's demise radiate across the ocean, most emphatically in a lesson to the Democratic Party. Bronx Congresswoman Alexandria Ocasio-Cortez's 11th hour recommendation of Corbyn, and the intertwining of Bernie Sanders's and Corbyn's staff, indicate that all Democrats who want to see the party thrive need to be alert against this synergy.")

Acknowledgements

Heartfelt thanks to Julie Blumenthal, Anthony Freda, Matt Taibbi, Catte Black, Kit Knightly, Tony Sutton, Mathias Bröckers, Angie Tibbs, John Stauber, Jeffrey St. Clair, Ron Unz, Diana Johnstone, Sietske Bergsma, Patrice Greanville, Lissa Johnson, Carey Weeks, Adam C. Madison, Hannah Rush, Maria Martinez, Shirley Fyfe, Nancy Volle, Flavia Westerwelle, J. David Bartram, Chris Farmer, Sage S. Johnston, Walter Broner, D. J. Richard, Sergey Zolotarev, Annette Baca, Michael McKay, Mark Brown, Judy Meinhold, Stella Ai, Meredith McElroy, Philip Baldwin, Anahita Mobarhan, Teri Cento, Jaap Greijdanus, D.C. MacKenzie, Paul Randall, Neil MacLeod, Alan Hodge, Alexis Viera, Don Gates, Zach Wheat, Blair Cummings, Kelley Lane, Colin McEvoy, Marjaleena Repo, S. A. Black, Kristin Kaul, Vernon Van Steenkist, Sean Hyland, John Bevan, David Marshall, Caitlin Johnstone, Robert Laine, Trina Shirk, Nico Dietel, John Bartram, Colleen McGuire, John Doores, Reg Tydell, Raymond Munro, Rob Murray, Eric Rasmussen, Van Foreman, Dimitrij Petkowski, Corey Twinney, Louis Haywood, Kenneth Goodman, Suellen Beverly, Kurtis Overkamp, Sean Carnohan, Andy Ward, Andrew Moynihan, John Read, Peter LaTona, Stan Smith, Sharon F. Crawford, Andrew Ward, Marjorie Mannos, Kurt Weithaler, Alan Rojer, Daniel Wirt, James Williamson, Josh Silver, Susie Kneedler, Fritz the Cat, Michael Denny, Susan Tinsley, Elliot Chen, Robert Kaplan, Kenneth Goodman, Richard Brooks, Michael L., Bob Martin, Kenneth Sabroff, Ard Vark, John R. Baker, Jr., Rob Burns, Kathy Woods, Chaz Donovan, Carol Ann Jones, Maximilien Robes, Richard Redei, Louis Haywood, Ann Pettus, Fabian Fabian, Larsen Gottschalk, D. Visentin, Antitermite, Louisa Jean Herd, Wayne J., Clarence Morrison, James Lipton, Sarah Hayes, Brendon Flynn, Spiritual Videos, Jakob Leistner, Micheal Denning, FreeAll.com, Aude Rain, Panagiotis Mantzivis, Göran Seth, David Weiss,

Michael Schwenk, Dan Blankinship, Ian Riley, Phillip Olley, Charilaos Zourelidis, Dan Schwabe, Marek N., Joerg Beringer, Kenneth Straus, Harriett Diller, Steve Gilmartin, Cat McGuire, John Clayden, Brett John, Thomas Wenzel, Pradeep Atluri, Michael Daniel, Simon Rook, Lex Marks, Corey Anderson Dansereau, Kim Wicker, Ulf Baukus, Claudio Schaefer, Ruth X., Philip Macfarlane, Crystal Faithe Kappel, Alex Zaretsky, Off-Guardian, ColdType, The Unz Review, Dissident Voice, ZeroHedge, CounterPunch, Greanville Post, Übersetzung aus dem Imperium, Entelekheia, Black Agenda Report, Rational Review, Signs of the Times, South Front, Tlaxcala, Le Grand Soir, Le Saker Francophone, The Automatic Earth, Come Don Chisciotte, Information Clearing House, The Fire, Linke Zeitung, ZNet, The Duran, Réseau International, OpEd News, The Fringe News, Vocidallestero, Titanic Lifeboat Academy, and everyone else who republished, translated, and otherwise supported the publication of these essays.

C. J. Hopkins is an award-winning playwright, novelist and political satirist. His plays have been produced and have toured internationally, playing theatres and festivals including Riverside Studios (London), 59E59 Theaters (New York), Belvoir St. Theatre (Sydney), Traverse Theatre (Edinburgh), the Du Maurier World Stage Festival (Toronto), Needtheater (Los Angeles), 7 Stages (Atlanta), English Theater Berlin, the Edinburgh Festival Fringe, Adelaide Fringe, the Brighton Festival, and the Noorderzon Festival (the Netherlands). His playwriting awards include the 2002 Best of the Scotsman Fringe Firsts (*Horse Country)*, the 2004 Best of the Adelaide Fringe (*Horse Country*), and a 2005 Scotsman Fringe First (*screwmachine/eyecandy*). His plays are published by Bloomsbury Publishing/Methuen Drama (UK) and Broadway Play Publishing, Inc. (US). His political satire and commentary has appeared in *CounterPunch*, *The Unz Review*, *ColdType*, *Off-Guardian*, *ZeroHedge*, *Dissident Voice*, and many other online journals and blogs, and has been widely translated. His debut novel, *Zone 23*, is published by Snoggsworthy, Swaine & Cormorant.

Also by C. J. Hopkins ...

"C. J. Hopkins is the rare writer who's so good at identifying uncomfortable truths that he essentially has to be removed from consideration for mass circulation. He's brave, original, enlightening, and hilarious, and his writing has an element of the forbidden that makes it even more fun."
- Matt Taibbi,
Rolling Stone

"Hopkins' ferociously funny yarn is not just a satire on our ever-worsening techno-dystopia ... in portraying individuals struggling and flailing against the uber-civilization around them like flies caught a spider web, *Zone 23* resonates with the great critiques of technological civilization."
- Kevin Barrett,
The Unz Review

Made in the USA
Monee, IL
15 June 2022

98087588R00108